Headteacher

To Julie Strevens (my wife), junior school teacher, for being with
me every step of the way – and being an incredible educator.
To Erin and Archie (my children) – for being amazing.
To John Botten (my dad), history teacher and educational
advisor – for teaching me the value of hard work and optimism.
To Anne Botten (my mum), reception teacher – for a lifetime
of service to the Early Years.
To Frank Birch (my grandfather), woodwork teacher – for teaching
me that you must always be led by your values, no matter the consequences.

To Neil, Jacqui, Soraya and Laura, the senior leaders at Emersons Green and
Blackhorse and an exceptional team of people – for your candour, occasional
forgiveness, humour, talent and friendship.
To Phil, ex-headteacher, Head of PD Leaf Trust – for thirty
years of chat about music and education.
To Ross, Faye, Ruth, Debbie, Sian and Claire, the executive team of The
Leaf Trust – for creating the Trust we always dreamed of.

Headteachering

A practical guide... with the messy bits left in

Simon Botten

BLOOMSBURY EDUCATION
LONDON OXFORD NEW YORK NEW DELHI SYDNEY

BLOOMSBURY EDUCATION
Bloomsbury Publishing Plc
50 Bedford Square, London WC1B 3DP, UK
Bloomsbury Publishing Ireland Limited
29 Earlsfort Terrace, Dublin 2, D02 AY28, Ireland

BLOOMSBURY, BLOOMSBURY EDUCATION and the Diana logo are trademarks of
Bloomsbury Publishing Plc

First published in Great Britain, 2025 by Bloomsbury Publishing Plc

This edition published in Great Britain, 2025 by Bloomsbury Publishing Plc

A catalogue record for this book is available from the British Library

ISBN: PB: 978-1-80199-708-9; ePub: 978-1-80199-709-6

2 4 6 8 10 9 7 5 3 1 (paperback)

Cover design by Adam Renvoize

Typeset by Newgen KnowledgeWorks Pvt. Ltd., Chennai, India
Printed and bound in the UK by CPI Group Ltd, CR0 4YY

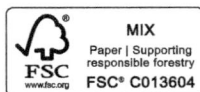

MIX
Paper | Supporting
responsible forestry
FSC
www.fsc.org   FSC® C013604

To find out more about our authors and books visit www.bloomsbury.com
and sign up for our newsletters

For product safety related questions contact productsafety@bloomsbury.com

Contents

Preface

'Simon, sorry to call you on your last day, but it's important we talk.'

The day had been a rollercoaster.

I had said my goodbyes to my colleagues at the school where I was deputy, and, having got home and changed, was just about to head out of my front door to meet them for my leaving do (karaoke and booze) when the phone rang.

It was the Chair of Governors at the school where I was starting as Head after the Easter break.

'Hi Reginald. I wasn't expecting you to call today, but what can I do for you?'

There was a pause.

'Well, Simon. The thing is...' His voice trailed off as he struggled to pick his words carefully, aware that his 'news' would surely expose the level of challenge which lay ahead.

'Four boys you see... I'm sure they didn't mean any real harm...'

Another pause.

'It's just that they *tried to burn down the school*...'

'And as you're really the new headteacher now...'

Another long pause.

'What should we do...?'

Introduction

Welcome to Headteachering

So you've made it to the threshold of headteachering? Well done! It's an amazing job and our schools need people just like you to lead them. You are going to be great!

Or alternatively...

You've not yet decided to have a go at headteachering, but you're tempted... A little voice in your head is telling you that this is something you should do. And so you should – it's never too soon to plot a course to headship – and we need people willing to step up and take on this role. You will get there, and when you do, you'll be great!

Or equally...

You are currently a headteacher and know a bit about headteachering already. If this is the case then I'm thinking that you'll know some of what I'm about to write about. But hopefully you'll find that this book resonates, and, if nothing else, it might help you to believe that you are on the right track. You are already doing the job brilliantly. Thank you for being great (and apologies for stating the obvious in places)!

This book is for all of you.

But this isn't 'that' book. You know the one – where a devastatingly good-looking and impossibly young super-head recounts walking into an inadequate school, saying a few inspirational things (with missionary confidence and zeal... perhaps about silent corridors and 'cog psych' and suchlike) and then finishing the year with an Outstanding Ofsted report and a knighthood.

Nor is it one of 'those' books. Where a devastatingly clever Oxford graduate recounts reading an impossible amount of educational research on leadership for their second PhD, whilst completing their first year as a Deputy, and then recounts how they *think* such research *could* be used as a headteacher. If they wanted to become one. Which they don't. Because they've just bagged a speaking tour to Dubai and a multi-format book deal.

Nor is it 'that other' book, where a truculent old-timer grumbles about the school system going to hell in a handcart whilst humble-bragging about their astonishing 'creative curriculum' based entirely on batik and interpretive dance (whilst failing to mention that many children leave the school being unable to read or write).

I am, sadly, not devastatingly handsome/clever, nor impossibly young. I don't have a knighthood, nor an 'Outstanding' school. I do not consider myself either a 'prog' (interpretive dance-led history lessons), nor a 'trad' (silent corridors and three months solitary confinement for forgetting a pen).

I do have 18 years of headteachering experience improving schools in difficulty, from a small failing church school, to a children's prison, to leading a school in crisis where the headteacher had recently been arrested and jailed. I have also stuck with leading a single school for 14 years, taking Blackhorse Primary from the bottom of the league tables to near the top, and leading it from being one of the least popular schools in Bristol to the second most over-subscribed. And then keeping it there.

This is a book which tells you why being a headteacher is the most important job you will ever do. Possibly the most important job in society. And definitely a job that you should either want to do (if you aren't yet) or should continue doing (if you already are).

This is the book which will help you see that, as headteacher, you hold a community by the hand; as headteacher, you don't just shape educational outcomes, but societal outcomes too. I have long believed that we headteachers have more power and control over the future of our society than any other civic office. Even Churchill knew it, quipping that *'Headmasters have powers at their disposal with which Prime Ministers have never yet been invested.'*

This book will show that headteachering is as hard as it is wonderful. That improving schools is the duty of all leaders, but is messy and fraught with self-doubt.

No other role allows you to shape the values and life-chances of tomorrow's society in such a way. Which is why it is so important that we should try to get the job right. And be quick to learn from our mistakes when we don't.

As well as my own reflections, this book will draw upon the wisdom and expertise of a range of experienced and successful headteachers. Each has a different story to tell, which they will share at the end of each chapter.

So let's start at the beginning, with some important thoughts on who you are as a headteacher.

Case Study: Keziah Featherstone

Executive headteacher, WomenEd co-founder, Headteachers' Roundtable member & author of *Punk Leadership*

Let's dump the illusion: there is *no* preparing for headship.

Sure, there are things that can get you relatively close to the reality but it's very approximate. Repeatedly you will look at your colleagues and utter something like 'this wasn't on the NPQH' and you'd be right. Nothing prepares you for a child bringing in their dead goldfish and attempting to launch a Viking funeral for it on the school pond; and, it is not every day you accidentally find a head of department in the store cupboard with a parent.

But that is what makes it the best job in the world.

Of course *you* can be a headteacher. Increasingly the cardboard cut-out model of headship is being abandoned: straight, middle-aged, white, authoritarian, cis-man, the so-called 'male, stale and pale'. This is not yet reflected in the data about the representation of women and people of colour within headship – but that's why we have to persevere and smash more of those ceilings down. Our children and our communities need it.

Without a doubt, headship is a challenging job; on occasion it's heart-breaking and it will feel exceptionally personal. But the opportunity to shape the culture of your school, how staff are treated and developed, how young people are valued, invested in and given opportunities to thrive, will always outweigh the negatives. Every criticism you have ever had about bad decisions or short-sighted strategy is now in your hands to shape and improve. It's not always easy, but it is always worth it.

Because every day will throw up bizarre and unimaginable moments to navigate, it is essential that you go into every interview as yourself and make no compromises. You do not want that level of responsibility if you are also hiding behind a mask of inauthenticity. You will be accepted for who you are, not a poor imitation of someone else, and that is the only way to lead. Not every school will want you but that is a *them* problem and you've just had a lucky escape.

Headship is an odd job. Pretty much every person in the world knows what one is and has their own memories of how they were treated by the ones they came across; pretty much every one of those people think they could do a better job than you but can't actually be bothered to get the qualifications and apply. You will not keep everyone happy and you shouldn't try to. It's a cliché, but always do the right thing, not the popular thing.

I am coming to the end of my second substantive headship and have held that role for ten years. As I move on to Trust leadership I can absolutely attest that there is nothing in the profession that comes close to headship. Staff will confide in you, share their most personal vulnerabilities and trust you to help, no matter what the problem. I'll never forget the time a teacher called me when his car wouldn't start, asking me how to fix it. The community will hold you in high esteem, believing you can fix everything from litter from a local chip-shop, to the punctuality of buses to getting them better social housing.

> But of course, the most wonderful moments are brought by the young people we work with: they are funny, clever, kind and thoughtful and will always remember you. Make those memories special!

Back to me and that moment of truth… My first day on the job…

I studied myself in the mirror of the gents and straightened my new Burtons tie.

This was my moment of self-actualisation. The moment where I would be crowned headteacher in front of the school: my first morning assembly with me at the helm.

I knew that every twitch, every facial expression would be studied by the staff who would shortly assemble with their classes. Every word would be imbibed with hidden meaning – whether it existed in reality or only in their perception.

I took a breath and walked into the empty hall.

Powerpoint presentation introducing myself? Check. *A natty mix of parable and personal anecdote – clear enough for the younger children to understand the key message of aspiration, but also laced with enough virtue-markers for staff, signalling what this new guy was about.*

Stirring music: Check. *Calming, yet contemporary – conveying that I was a cool guy who didn't mind playing popular music in a church school assembly.*

I placed myself at the front. *Assertive, yet friendly body stance? Check!*

All was ready.

First to arrive were the Infants… bit noisy… probably just excited to meet their new headteacher…

Their staff looked embarrassed but not surprised.

'Thank you to everyone who has come in silently,' I announced.

A few children took the cue. Many didn't.

Moments later the older children piled in. Pushing, talking loudly.

'Thank you again to everyone who has come in silently,' I repeated, my armour of 'assertive yet friendly body stance' starting to creak.

Finally, the Year 6s bowled in.

These, the school's oldest children, knew exactly how to make an entrance. Shouts, laughs, pushes… and a swagger which left little doubt who they thought was in charge.

Time slowed.

I knew that if I was to have any hope of charting a new course for this school – which I'd already been told was on its knees – then I'd have to make a stand. Right here, right now… in front of all the staff and all the children.

'Excuse me, Year 6,' I enunciated assertively, 'I would like you to stop and walk in quietly.'

A boy stopped dead in front of me and smiled. I felt a room full of eyes assessing the scene, knowing (unlike the new headteacher) that this was the same boy who had recently been caught setting fire to the Elliot building.

He stopped talking and looked me dead in the eye. The other Year 6s stopped talking too.

They just needed a headteacher to be firm… firm and relatable… and young… and cool… don't forget cool (I had an earring)!

'Fuck off!' he replied.

Chapter 1
Your first 100 days as a headteacher

Learning to swim in a storm

I remember every detail of my first day as a headteacher. Whether your first headship or your fifth, those early days in a new school are exciting and terrifying in equal measure.

And this is where the role of headteacher differs from all others.

You see, any other member of staff has the time and space to quietly grow into the role, supported by colleagues who know the school and what it is trying to achieve. And whilst elements of this are true for the headteacher, you are also expected to be the leader from day one, and as such, your decisions and words and actions (big or small) are scrutinised by the entire community.

The impression which you make in those first 100 days, along with the decisions you make, will dictate how quickly the staff, pupils and community come to trust you. Moreover, if you are leading a school that requires rapid improvement, then the momentum you seek is locked within the choices you make and the messages you convey within those first two months.

It is therefore worth spending some time thinking about.

Surprisingly, given the accepted importance for all leaders of their first 100 days in office, very little research has been done into how leaders can use this time effectively. I first wrote about this some years ago (Botten, 2017), and it has since been blogged about by the brilliant David Carter (2019) amongst other writers. However, there is no academic research on this important period, but, having started leading in new schools a number of times (I'm told successfully) I do think the following areas provide some pointers on what to do…

1. Do your homework

There will have been a good few months between getting the job as headteacher and starting the role. It is important to use this time to find out as much as possible about the school you are about to lead.

Some information will be freely available on the internet (Ofsted reports, published performance data and any news articles about the school) and the school's website will also give you a good understanding of how the school promotes its current curriculum, vision and values. You should also ask for any formal SEF documents, copies of headteacher reports to Governors/Trustees and any school improvement planning, although schools are under no obligation to make these documents available, so tact and respect in communication is key during this transition period.

You should also have plenty of opportunities to visit the school and start to get a feel for the main strengths and weaknesses. This too requires tact as it is the previous headteacher's school until the day before you start and how much access you get will be for them to decide. Most outgoing headteachers try to do all they can to support the new incumbent by allowing them to spend time with the school's middle leaders and walking them through an honest self-evaluation. But, again, this can vary hugely from school to school.

Sometimes, getting access to the school prior to starting the role is more difficult. This was the case with my first headship (the one with the Year 6 fire-starter). The previous headteacher had resigned abruptly before I started and the governors, a little panicked by events in the school and a ropey Ofsted, were keen not to 'scare me off', so limited my access to things which painted the school in an unforgiving light. Therefore the opportunities to visit were limited – as was access to documents. If this is the case, approach the LA or Trust as they should be able to facilitate the handover of information so that you can start to gather intel.

But the more you know about the school before you start, gathered from as many sources as possible, the better.

2. Consider your key messages for the first day/week/month

A change of leadership can be a disconcerting moment for a school community. Whether the previous head was successful and loved, or whether the school is failing and in trouble with Ofsted, staff and parents can find it a confusing time as the certainties of the past (good or bad) start to erode.

Whenever I start as a new leader I therefore carefully consider which three key messages I'm going to communicate over the first day, the first week and across the first 100 days.

These messages will be entirely context-dependent and will look very different at each school. For example, if the school is already 'Good', with a strong reputation and popular outgoing Head, then my key messages are likely to be based around my vision for education and how it dovetails with the school's existing vision. However, if you are taking over a school in difficulty, then your messaging may have to be more assertive and direct.

My first school as Head was at risk of special measures and had behaviour which was preventing effective teaching and learning. Learning environments were also unloved and the school was a mess. My messages were therefore all about my expectations about behaviour and the need for a tidy environment (as a proxy for how the school feels about itself).

When working with staff at Emersons Green Primary, where I started as Executive Headteacher in September 2022, the messages were quite different again. The school was 'Good' but fearful of a 'hostile takeover' by the other bigger, and higher-profile Blackhorse Primary, which I'd led since 2011. The messages I constantly repeated here were therefore all about 'two equally strong and successful schools working together in equal partnership'.

Once you have decided on these key messages, repeat them often – and to all stakeholders. Make a point of weaving them into idle conversations with staff and parents alike at every opportunity.

Say it once and it is a passing comment – say it 100 times and it becomes a mantra.

And a mantra will allow a jittery staff team to know exactly what you are focused on during those first 100 days.

3. Create formal opportunities to clearly communicate these messages

It is a difficult balancing act, especially in an already successful school, to know how visible and dominant you should be as the new headteacher. Go in too gung-ho and you will immediately raise the heckles of staff whose support you will shortly rely on. Be too passive and staff will be confused about your leadership priorities and will attempt to fill this vacuum.

As the new headteacher, you ideally want your first day to be an INSET, where you can gather all the staff – and I mean *all* (site staff, cleaners, admin, support – everyone) – and let them know what you stand for and what your key messages are.

Follow this with events for parents, both in the evening and after school drop-off in the morning, where you can introduce yourself and reiterate your key messages.

Assemblies (like the one I'd planned which was somewhat 'challenging') are another opportunity to show who you are and set an ambitious narrative. And remember, whilst these are primarily for the children, the staff are also a bonus audience. Indeed, two years into my first headship a staff member confided that in the early days she needed to hear the aspirational and hopeful messages I'd pump out to the children at every assembly just as much as the children did!

4. Find out why the school exists

The first thing I ask when I start working with any new setting is 'why does this school exist?'

And at your first INSET day, this is as good a place to start as any.

We'll discuss this key question extensively in the next chapter, but it is a question which you should aim to find the answer to within the first 100 days. Where the vision is strong, the stakeholders will be able to answer this question with ease. If this is the case, you will need to tread carefully as rubbishing a highly valued existing vision can be deeply offensive to the team, who may have worked hard over many years to form it.

More often, when you ask staff this question, they will give you a range of interconnected thoughts and ideas which have a common theme but are ill-defined. They know the main themes of the school, but not how they are operationalised. This is the most common response because most schools don't truly live their visions every moment of every day. This doesn't necessarily mean the school is bad or failing, only that it has not yet defined its true 'self'. In this case, it will be your job to bring this existing successful vision and culture into the light – but not on your first day! Or even on your first 100 days – these you will use to try to understand the vision that is currently hiding in the brickwork.

Whatever range of answers you get, it is important not to immediately pass judgement on how well a school can describe its purpose. Sometimes staff are just a bit shy and tongue-tied by this new leader in their midst. We also have to check our own biases at this point as just because somewhere else we worked believed in a certain vision, or because you have strong opinions on X or Y, it does not necessarily mean that this is right for your new school.

Spend these first 100 days truly understanding what the school thinks it exists to do. It will give you a sense of how well the school knows itself – and what might need to come next.

5. Find out what each staff member thinks

Whilst this is easier in a small primary with 30 staff than a large secondary with 200, meeting with as many staff as possible 1-on-1 is essential to really start understanding the school.

I preferred to block out whole days (with a roving supply teacher to cover) to hold these 20 minute meetings, whilst David Carter (2019) suggests holding one each day. These meetings aren't compulsory (some staff just want to watch and wait whilst they work you out) so staff are free to sign up or not.

At these meetings I asked the same two questions:

1. What would you like me to know about you and the school?
2. What do you think I need to focus on?

I caveated these questions with the understanding that I might not be able or willing to act on the information I'd been given, but it still helped me to know what people think.

I have found these meetings invaluable as it is amazing how candid and insightful people can be when asked directly. I also find some nice biscuits and a cup of tea goes a long way to punctuate the meeting during a long day of teaching.

6. Find out what the parents think

Whilst I wouldn't recommend conducting formal surveys of parents in the first 100 days, as I believe these can feel a bit impersonal, gathering anecdotal views on the school can help you understand how the parental community feels.

Being visible out on the playground every morning and evening is essential for school leaders for a myriad of reasons which we'll explore later, but it also allows you to wander up to groups of parents (more easily in primary school where they drop off every day), introduce yourself and ask them, much like the staff, whether there is anything they'd like to say about the school. Whilst it can feel agonisingly awkward to strike up conversations with parents (who may eye you with deep suspicion) this will provide a vital perspective on how the school is seen, especially if you make a point to talk to a wide range of parents – not just the ones who smile at you!

Likewise, parent coffee mornings and information evenings are another good way to engage with parents early on, although I would counsel against having an open agenda with a large group of parents if the school is in difficulty. Whether it was your fault or not, there is a real chance that an angry mob will form and you'll find yourself fielding questions which you currently have no answers to. A better approach is to have an evening meeting where you introduce yourself, explain your background and past achievements, and then share (at this point in general terms) what your educational philosophy is, making careful effort to align it – at least in part – with any strongly held existing ethos or vision.

7. Find out what the children think

This is as essential as finding out what the parents and staff think, and in some ways a whole lot simpler, as children will tell you the unvarnished truth pretty much straight away. This can either be formally through meetings with the school council or asking older children to take you for a tour of the school, but also informally by taking playground duties and sitting with the children in the dining hall at lunchtime.

8. Get into class as soon as you can

This is another area where you really need to be clear about 'starting as you mean to go on'. At the very first staff meeting in the school where I'm now Executive Headteacher, I made it very clear that, whilst my role was different to the Head of School's, I am extremely interested in supporting them to become great teachers, and as such, I would be dropping into class at least once a week to gain an understanding as to how teaching and learning works at the school. Ideally, this should be done with other senior and middle leaders who can narrate how teaching and curriculum is organised across the school.

Importantly, when you first go into a teacher's classroom, try to smile. Even if the teaching you are seeing is not what you'd hope for, keep any feedback for another time (unless something is dangerous or inappropriate). These first couple of visits are simply to take the temperature of learning across the school and to start to build trust with the staff. There'll be time enough for feedback once you've established a routine.

Better still, roll your sleeves up and help out as a teaching assistant in the class for a few minutes. I'm told I partly got the job at Blackhorse (where I've been Head for 14 years) because in between interview tasks I went and played trains on the carpet in Reception with a group of children in my best three-piece suit! Remember, teachers will be making judgements about you during these visits to their classrooms as much as you will be making judgements of them.

But make the intent and purpose of these drop-ins clear from the outset – so that there are no surprised faces when you turn up at the door.

9. Set the culture within your Senior Leadership Team

I believe that headteachers get the leadership teams which they deserve. You only get one opportunity to set the tone in your leadership team meetings and ensure that communication is open and solution-focused.

Brené Brown, in her excellent book *Dare to Lead* (2018 – a must-read for any first-time headteacher), talks extensively about creating such a culture – something which is often overlooked in the clamour to 'get stuff done'. She talks about 'container building', sometimes called 'contracting', where the team define how it will work at a psychological level. She suggests teams should seek to answer the following questions:

What do you need to show up and do the work?

What will get in the way of you showing up and doing the work?

What does support look like?

This can all feel 'a bit American' to us Brits. But having done this numerous times when forming new leadership teams, I have concluded that 'setting the rules for the psychological safety and effectiveness of the team' makes a huge difference. It gives explicit permission for team members to speak freely, even if this involves sharing an opinion different to your own, and also creates a boundary to prevent unhelpful or undermining behaviours by calling these out before they happen.

Again, whilst this can be done at any time as a headteacher, it is most easily done as a brand new headteacher as it sets the tone going forward.

I also firmly believe that you must expressly give permission for your leaders to question your decisions openly in these team meetings. If you don't get honest feedback as to how you are performing and how decisions which you are making are being received, then (especially in these early days) you run the very real risk of a misstep causing serious waves – something you don't need when you are trying to build trust and alliances. Don't get me wrong, I don't mean for one minute you should bend to the will of your SLT at every occasion. But you should try to make informed choices based on the best information possible.

10. Teach

Whilst you may have left the classroom behind in this new role, I think it sends a powerful message when a headteacher does some teaching, again, especially in those early days.

It shows the staff that you can do the very thing which you are asking of them. It shows the children that you are all about teaching and it shows the parents that you are interested in their children. We'll discuss this more in a later chapter, but, even if it's just for an hour or so every few weeks (or a booster group, etc.) this will show the team that you're serious about teaching and learning more than anything else.

11. Create a 100-day development plan

Whilst you may have inherited a fully written School Development Plan, and most likely a 3-4 year Strategic Plan which is partially completed, it is worth creating a short plan which covers your first term as headteacher. The reason for this is that you start with a wafer-thin evidence base on which to make judgements about where to focus school improvement work. There may be a glaring hole in particular data or a recent inspection report which gives you a clear starting point, but equally (and more commonly) it will be very unclear as to what needs doing to improve the school in your first few weeks.

Your plan should therefore include much of what we've so far discussed, plus any focused school evaluation activities which you want to prioritise. A 100-day RAP (again more on this later) will be a very useful tool in ensuring all the pieces of school improvement work get done and aren't crowded out by the constant 'white noise' of 'stuff' that could fill your every day if you're not careful.

12. Secure a quick win

An important element of this initial 100-day plan should be a positive action which shows that you have the power and determination to get something done! Again, this will depend on where the school is on its improvement journey (please don't go upending things in a good school as this will really piss people off), so think carefully what this might be. It could just be tidying and organising an unloved corner of the school. It might be introducing a new way for the children to line up (if this is a problem). Make sure it's something which is likely to have widespread support and (importantly) is something which is relatively easy to achieve successfully.

13. Watch your language – and that of others

The language you use or accept from others around school defines the professional standards adopted by the whole school team. Professor Tim Brighouse talks about this power of language in his excellent book *Essential Pieces – The Jigsaw of a Successful School* (2006). If you allow yourself to moan and be negative around colleagues, don't be surprised when they do the same.

Conversely, positive and ambitious language can have a huge impact on staff morale and expectations. Just as repeating key messages over and over again helps these messages to be internalised, using language which underscores the confidence which you have in the team's ability will go a long way. Even when the school is in difficulty, selecting language which depersonalises any failures but personalises any successes will give staff a boost when they face an uncertain future.

But there is one thing you must **absolutely not** say:

'At my last school we...'

Nothing will piss off your new colleagues more quickly than you constantly comparing them to your previous school. Especially as you will not be able to hide the fact that (in not knowing or understanding your new school at this point) you are likely to secretly believe that everything your previous school did was better. This unconscious bias must be avoided at all cost – and certainly not given voice to!

*

So what happened to the sweary Year 6?

'Fuck off!'

Time stopped.

Now, I would love to tell you a story about a brave and self-confident leader who took decisive action then and there, suspending the child in front of 210 onlookers – thus sending a powerful message about what behaviour I'd accept.

But I'd been a headteacher about two hours.

Sure, I sent the child out of the hall with a member of staff and an internal school punishment was meted out and parents called etc.

But I didn't have the bottle to suspend a child on my first day (now I would have done so in a heartbeat).

I did however learn this lesson fast. The behaviour around school was out of control and children challenged teachers constantly and with impunity (more of this later).

By the end of my first 100 days I had suspended 20 children. By the second term I had only needed to suspend two. By the end of my second year, I didn't need to suspend children at all.

But that's a story for later.

*

Let's look at some advice and experiences from Dr Kulvarn Atwal, a courageous and values-led leader who explains how he used his first 100 days to demonstrate to the whole community his approach to both the community and to learning.

Case Study: Dr Kulvarn Atwal

Executive Head Teacher at Highlands Primary School & Uphall Primary Schools (London), author of *The Thinking School* and *The Thinking Teacher*

In the first 100 days as a headteacher it is vitally important to respect the context of the school community that you are leading, and to spend as much time listening as you do talking. As outlined by Simon, when I take on a new school, I ensure that I have individual meetings with each member of the staff team to gain a deeper understanding of their personal perspectives. You want them to be authentically open and honest with you. In the same way you take time to get to know each individual student when you get a new class, I look at the staff team in the same way. It is important to develop your own perspective of the staff team rather than relying solely on the views of current/previous leaders at the school. Remember that you are going to be spending every minute espousing and articulating your values. The aim is for every member of staff in the school to be aligned in their core values.

If your staff and children share a strong sense of core values, they behave in a way which supports good learning for all. The first action I take when I begin at a new school is to become a Unicef Rights Respecting School. One core outcome is that the staff and children have a shared language when it comes to the behaviour and rights of people in our learning community. Children do not behave in a way because the teacher has told them to and teachers do not behave in a way because the headteacher has told them to. I provide an environment that gives all staff a voice and the opportunity to co-construct knowledge. Teachers do something because it is the right thing to do. In those first 100 days, consider the extent to which the actions of staff at your school reflect their espoused values. To what extent do we do what we actually say we do, and how well do these actions reflect our values? Giving everyone a voice, to express both positive and negative viewpoints, helps to build trust within the workplace. When you embed high trust within the culture and fabric of the school, it will serve to liberate people to: share their areas for development; be creative and take risks; learn and grow; and enable others around them to learn and grow.

Build an environment in which there is both high challenge and high trust. The more we trust each other, the more we are able to open up our practice and the more we are able to challenge each other. The difficulty with many teams in schools is the lack of open challenge. People feel that they cannot challenge, because it will be taken personally or negatively. Challenge is accepted if the team members share common values and goals. In my first year of headship, I wanted to introduce a strategy that was initially viewed by staff with suspicion. I met with team leaders to explain that I wanted each teacher to send each child's English or maths book home, accompanied with a dialogue sheet designed to engage the parents in a learning conversation with their children. My rationale was that children would really value an opportunity to share their learning at home, and that it would support parental engagement.

I was given every excuse under the sun as to why it would be a bad idea, including: why bother as parents wouldn't complete the sheet; the books would never come back; parents would question the quality of the work, marking or teaching; and even that the parents were illiterate! I won't go through all my responses but I will share my response to the potential criticism from parents of children's work and marking. If the quality of the children's learning and teacher marking isn't good enough for parents, then it shouldn't be good enough for us. Alternatively, if it is unwarranted criticism, we should value the opportunity to engage with parents to share views. On meeting with team leaders, I made sure that I listened to all the views and fears shared. I explained that I thought it was a good idea and would be fine if I was proved wrong. I asked them to commit whole-heartedly to having a trial of the process, and that we would collectively evaluate the process. If everybody didn't want to continue with it, we would stop.

This conversation was positive because it removed the potential discord. We were all committed to engaging authentically in the process and evaluating its relative success. I clearly demonstrated my values in this example. I implemented a strategy that valued parental voice and engagement in their children's learning. I wanted to develop a stronger learning partnership between the school and the home. I discussed the need to value our children's learning by having the highest expectations for standards in our books. I demonstrated that I was prepared to be innovative, creative and take risks. I had already discussed it with two key leaders responsible for inclusion and parental engagement and they were in full agreement – this demonstrated my commitment to working in collaboration. I also demonstrated that I genuinely valued staff voice and would be prepared to revise my opinion if necessary.

I also hoped to be demonstrating learning-focused leadership of staff and children. The result, through the leadership of teachers, was a huge success with an average return in each class of over 90% of the dialogue sheets, and it was an activity that set the standard for our future work and success. Many years later, we continue to send the books home once each term. This example demonstrates when challenge was accepted and served to build trust. Put simply, children's learning is at the centre, underpinned by teacher learning. Our values reflected this and informed our actions.

Dr Atwal's example is a brilliant one: it shows how you can implement an idea within your first 100 days which states your intent and purpose for the future without upending everything straight away, and shows how to bring others along with you. He balances his authentic values-led leadership with a deep desire to build a learning community comprising the views of both staff and parents. His track-record in improving schools is a testament to how successful this approach has been.

Key takeaways

1. Think carefully how you present yourself on Day 1 – all eyes will be looking for clues as to your character and intent.

2. Find out what the school perceives its core purpose to be. What does it stand for? How does it define itself? What historical school events have defined it?

3. Using this information, settle on three key messages which define your priorities and beliefs. Repeat these messages often throughout your first 100 days.

4. Listen to everyone. Create opportunities to talk to the children, staff and parents, both formally and informally.

5. Set the culture of your leadership team at your very first meeting. You'll get only one natural chance to do this!

6. Smile – a lot.

Reflection tasks

These can be used either in starting a new school, or when starting a new school year.

What are your first impressions about the school? Write down the first five words that come into your head, completing the table below:

First five words that come to mind	Evidence for these

Search your school on the internet. Look at the first five pages of results (discounting ones which link to the school's own website). What does this tell you about the school and how it is perceived in the community?

_____

_____

_____

_____

_____

What key message do you want to give to the staff/ parents/ children on Day 1? How will you communicate this?

_____

_____

_____

_____

_____

What three key messages do you want to communicate to parents in your first newsletter?

_____

_____

_____

_____

_____

_____

Complete the table below.

Most pressing priorities:	Consistent message you intend to give around these:
1.	
2.	
3.	

Chapter 2

Creating a compelling vision

Why does your school exist?

'I think we need to start to consider whether we need to change the name of the school...'

The Chair of Governors looked solemn. The other governors shuffled in their seats, acutely aware that this was my first meeting with them as substantive headteacher and the reputation of the school was considered so poor that members of the governing body were actively discussing irradiating a school name which had existed for over half a century.

The school should have been full. The building was less than seven years old and benefited from all the mod-cons you'd expect. It was a world away from the school I'd just left – a 50s modular build where you could poke your finger through the wooden wall panels, and the heating system ran, I think, on burning old tyres in a furnace under the hall.

Sadly, at the time (April 2011), Blackhorse was one of the least popular schools not just in the area, but in the whole county. It had slumped to near the bottom of the SATs league tables and only 17 families had chosen the school for their children in the new Reception intake (of 60 places).

And whilst I'd been working, alongside the excellent acting HT Phil Winterburn, with the school for well over a year to keep it out of special measures (the sole target given to us by the LA), Phil securing an unexpected 'Good' inspection grade just before I started as the substantive head after Easter (more on this later), the work had been focused entirely on 'emergency school improvement' – ensuring the quality of basic teaching was up to scratch.

The school badly needed to improve its reputation and set a more ambitious course for the future.

You see, despite having been in existence since the 1950s, Blackhorse had only existed on its current site since 2004, having moved a mile from its original site on the Blackhorse estate (consisting of 60s social housing), onto the new site on the newly built Emersons Green estate, doubling in size to become (hopefully) a two-form entry school.

And it was at this point in its history that the school lost itself. It had been used to being a small school on a small council estate; this it knew how to do. Being a big school, serving a big new housing development, as well as the original estate…? This it did not know how to do. And so it drifted on the currents of fate, being buffeted by whatever circumstances blew in.

'So, Simon… what do you think? Change the name? That should get people's attention!'

I looked around the room at the group. They were good people, desperate for their school to become what we all knew it should be.

'Why does this school exist?' I asked them.

There was a moment of silence, followed by a slightly uncomfortable mumbling about standards…

Then silence.

The answer to our problem was that simple. As a community – we simply didn't know.

*

The power of vision

I am of the opinion that a school's vision is the single most important statement in determining whether a school will be amazing, or whether it will simply be… well… 'fine' … 'ordinary'…

Every school I've ever visited has a vision statement.

And nearly all of them are crap.

Now, I'm not being rude and provocative for the sake of it. I'm sure most schools have a perfectly lovely vision statement… perhaps laminated… or even put in a clip frame in the foyer…

But does it really determine every choice they make as a school?

Whilst in some schools this is absolutely the case, in most I would argue that the vision statement is, at best, underdeveloped, and, at worst, largely ignored.

Done well, a school vision can unite the whole community around a common purpose. It acts as an accelerant to nearly all school improvement activity as, when people know and agree on a higher purpose which extends beyond operational matters, they tend to offer far more discretionary effort than they would if they were simply concerned with 'task completion'. A compelling vision provides us with a sense of quest and adventure. Of striving for something worthy of our best endeavours. It lifts our work as educators up from 'only' the business of teaching to the business of changing lives.

It is not that most schools don't have a sense of what they are trying to achieve in their vision statement. I have never seen a vision statement that didn't try to articulate what the school was trying to achieve. It is more that most vision statements are clumsy and bloated. They are long and wordy and complicated. And so most schools write them, but then struggle to live them, for these reasons, resulting in them becoming a tick box exercise, instead of a shining beacon in the distance which draws all eyes and efforts towards it.

So, if our school vision is the driver of all other school improvement (and it is), then it is important we spend some time getting it right...

Our vision is part origin story and part quest

If we are to tell a compelling story then we must know the plot.

Unless your school is brand new, many other school leaders will have gone before you and there will be a history to the school which you ignore at your peril.

When trying to improve the school where I was first headteacher, I tried and (as a very young and inexperienced headteacher) failed to persuade the staff to part with the school's Victorian motto '*To study is to learn*'. To this day I don't really know what it meant, but it was totemic to the staff who saw my attempts to change and modernise a school with 150 years of history as an attack on the generations of educators who had gone before.

When articulating a school's vision it is therefore important to first consider your school's 'origin story'. Much like Batman or the Incredible Hulk, schools arrive at a particular moment in time as a result of things that have gone before. I have seen many headteachers lose the goodwill of staff and the community by ignoring the past and only forging on with a bright (and baggage-free) future.

A school's visioning exercise is both origin story (what went before) and quest (a distant shore to strike for).

It is also useful at this point to consider what is influencing your philosophy of education, as this will in turn influence the ambitious future for the school which the re-visioning process will seek to capture.

At Blackhorse, our thinking in 2011 was heavily influenced by the publication of Doug Lemov's *Teach like a Champion* (2010), Matthew Syed's *Bounce* (2011) and, later on, Angela Duckworth's *Grit* (2016). These books fired our interest in the notion that talent is a myth, that resilience can be taught and that 'champions are built not born'. Again, by being clear about our influences right at the beginning of the visioning process, it was then easier to create an authentic and coherent vision.

So spend some time understanding your school's origin story and be clear in the core beliefs or concepts that are driving your ambition for the future, before you begin trying to formulate a school vision.

Why does your school exist?

You now need to answer this simple question.

As mentioned in the previous chapter, the first question that I ask any school when I begin supporting them with school improvement appears so simple: Why does this school exist?

And yet, many (probably most), school leaders struggle to answer it.

Many will talk about standards and outcomes and curriculum and their values and suchlike, and it's clear that they have a good understanding of the 'how' and 'what'… but rarely the 'why'.

When you ask most school leaders what their school's 'why' is, they will immediately start telling you about educating children – the 'why' of every school in the land. But very few will tell you why their school exists, and differs from all those around it.

However, I have come across a small number of schools who can do this without skipping a beat. These schools fire out a clipped and precise definition of their purpose which captures their long-term hopes and dreams for every pupil within the school. These schools view their vision (their 'why') as the foundation stone for everything they do.

In Simon Sinek's excellent book *Start with Why: How great leaders inspire everyone to take action* (2009), he looks at how the most successful businesses across the world first define their 'why' before going on to define their 'what' and their 'how'.

So as school leaders, we must do better at defining our 'why'.

Importantly, this 'why' shouldn't just describe the 'here and now'. Our vision should be forever slightly out of reach. Touchable, but never fully attainable in the present, as a fully attainable vision lacks ambition and just seeks to maintain the status quo – which comes with its own dangers. The best visions are coloured by the present but nod to brighter days on distant shores.

Yet defining our 'why' is easier said than done.

On the surface, schools (in the UK at least) are very similar. We teach broadly the same curriculum; we follow broadly the same national policies; we teach broadly the same way. However, ask any school what makes it different – its 'Unique Selling Point' – and you start to open up a deeper discussion about its 'why'. At this point schools start to introduce thoughts about their distinct character; things which are highly specific to their community and setting. Often some of these may have found their way into the school's vision/mission statement. But, as often, they will be ill-defined and woolly. They will be seen as mere 'colour' and not the very essence of the vision itself.

To understand our 'why' we need to start by asking as many people as possible why the school exists. This exercise, if done solely by the SLT and devoid of community input, will almost certainly fail, as the community will feel that they have been frozen out of 'their' school's future. Asking as many people as possible will ensure that everyone feels heard. It will also elicit a huge number of disparate responses, reflecting individuals' personal relationships with the school. But, ask the question enough times, and, clusters of 'whys' will start emerging. These will usually reflect the 'here and now' and lack the future ambition for the school, which is something which you as a leader need to champion as a concept amongst the staff.

Your skill as leader will be to take the school community's core beliefs 'in the now' and add to them the ambition which you seek for the future. This future thinking will be a careful balancing act and will depend on the circumstances in which the school finds itself at the time of re-visioning. For instance, if your school is already wildly successful with a long and prestigious history to draw upon, then you may wish to include tradition as the key ingredient and augment this with future ambition. However, if your school is not thriving and if there is no long sense of successful tradition (as tradition should not be canonised if it stunts progress), then, whilst you will need to refer back to what went before, most of the 'why' will be based in future aspirations.

Having gathered all these ideas and hopes for a brighter future, it is not enough to cobble these together in long-form and pin them up in the staff room. For schools to truly define their 'why', they then need to boil these ideas down until they can be expressed in one simple line.

Not a paragraph with lots of long and, very impressive sounding, educational buzz-words.

One line.

Here's some thoughts from Simon Smith on his school's origin story and the questions which he asked, and continues to ask, the school's stakeholders in order to ensure that the school's vision is the driver of all school improvement.

Case Study: Simon Smith

Headteacher and children's reading champion, East Whitby Primary

Currently I'm a headteacher of a school that is 70 years old. Its existence isn't down to me or the people in the building. It's here because when it was built, the east side of our town needed a primary school; it was back in the days where there was only one bridge and the expansion of the town meant more schools were needed. It was envisioned as a true community space, a place for the people on this side of town. Building-wise we have a full stage, curtains, backdrops, and the hall even has holes in the wall where a cinema projector used to sit. It was a school built in its make-up to represent its community and that is still a fiercely stubborn streak that runs through the very DNA of our school.

When we look at our vision and values, the starting point is almost never a blank slate. Every school carries the history of the space, the people, the community. Some of that is good, and some of that is bad but it is always there. However, for school leaders, our starting point should always be around the young people who walk in the doors. What are our hopes, our ambitions for them?

Vision isn't short-term. I look at our school now and it's the product of that vision I set out in an interview on a snowy February morning back in 2014. Whilst the school has morphed and changed from what it was to what it is now, the core of that vision very much guides the everyday.

It's not just mine, the kernel; the starting was mine and very much sat in my beliefs and values, but the vision was created together, staff, pupils, stakeholders, community.

We discussed, we challenged, to create that vision for our school. That vision should not be the same as the school down the road because we are not them and the vision is a statement of us.

So we set it out, we asked questions, we listened and finally we created.

There are lots of ways to do this but we found these questions a good starting point.

- What are your goals for our students, staff, and community?
- What sets our school apart from others?
- What do we believe?
- What unites our school?
- What makes us… us?

The clarity of the vision, whatever that may be, is the guiding principle. From that vision your values, your expectations, literally everything flows. It is the 'what' of your school. It is the direction of travel, the drive, the relentless push. It provides clarity and purpose, guiding strategic decisions around curriculum, priorities, resource allocation, and progress monitoring. An effective vision rallies and motivates staff, students, parents, the wider community.

However, the problem with vision is that it can be woolly and fuzzy; it can be an amorphous blob of vibes, a feelgood factor but without clarity. 'I want every child to…'. Platitudes without substance and no direction to get there.

The Education Endowment Foundation (EEF) highlights several key recommendations for developing an effective school vision. Having an effective school vision is the first step to cohesive school improvement:

> *Involve a range of stakeholders. Engage staff, governors, parents and students in the process to build buy-in and ownership. Gather input on core values and priorities.*
>
> *Focus on learning and quality first teaching. The vision should encapsulate high aspirations for student outcomes and learning. It should motivate continuous improvement.*
>
> *Be ambitious and achievable. Strike a balance between ambitious goals and realistic expectations. The vision should stretch the school community outside its comfort zone but still be attainable.*
>
> *Align vision with values and ethos. The vision should reflect the school's key values and priorities. It should shape the school's culture and identity.*
>
> *Keep it simple and clear. A good vision statement is concise, memorable, and inspires action. Avoid vague or overly complex language.*
>
> *Review and revisit. Evaluate how well the vision is driving school improvement. Be willing to revisit and revise the vision as needed to keep it fresh and relevant.*
>
> *Model and embed in practice. School leadership must demonstrate the values.*

Whilst I don't think anyone would disagree with this, vision is perhaps more, it's overarching, it doesn't sway with the educational breeze. The vision is a statement of the leaders that created it. There may be different ways to get there but the core of it, the truth of it doesn't falter. The vision is ultimately the core. It is the thing that helps you make the tough decisions.

Every decision stems from that vision. Everything is an extension of that. Your policies, your systems, the routines, how you staff, where you prioritise your spending. Ultimately it goes all the way down to the teaching in the classroom. Everyone should know it, it should sing in your space, people should feel it and believe it.

So the questions are therefore:

- What is your school about?
- What is your vision?
- Does everyone know it?

> If not, it's not a vision, it's an idea. A vision is a something communicated, it leads the way, it provides support in the challenging times, it helps us celebrate our successes, it provides the map and compass for our decisions and it helps us be ever looking forward. Vision is a restless beast that is never satisfied and all our schools are better for that.

One line

Tell me everything your school stands for in under six words.

Most commonly, a school's vision statement will be long and wordy. It will have been created either many years earlier (and then largely ignored), or it will have been created by committees of staff and governors, each adding another layer of complexity so that school leaders have to spend ten minutes explaining what it means to prospective parents.

To paraphrase Mark Twain: *'I apologise for such a long vision statement – I didn't have time to write a short one.'*

And if it is long and wordy, then I would suggest it is almost certainly pointless.

You see, if your vision is what guides your school improvement decisions (and it should), then people need to be able to remember it. Right now – right this very moment – pick up your phone and text some friendly staff members and ask them to recite the school's vision statement. I guarantee that if your statement is more than 20 words, then almost nobody will be able to tell you what it is.

They might be able to talk around it in general terms. But they won't be able to recite it with absolute clarity, which matters if you are to use this statement as the core belief from which all school decisions stem.

So your next step is one of the hardest: capture the whole essence of the school's vision for the future in as few words as possible. There is no shortcut to this. It will need to sit on big bits of paper on working walls in the staffroom for weeks whilst the core of its meaning is thrashed out.

At Blackhorse, our vision is to 'Build champion learners'. It seeks to embody the creation of young people who have an absolute unwavering belief in their own ability to overcome obstacles and succeed in life; of young people who are captains of their own destiny; who make their own luck! It was also a direct challenge to the passive attitudes and low ambition which afflicted the school in 2011, when, at the bottom of the league tables, such bold words sounded like a forlorn hope.

But it changed the narrative.

It gradually seeped into the minds, firstly, of the staff, and then of the children, and then of the parents. It became the shorthand for what we wanted our children to be.

It was deliberately 'tabloid' in its meaning. There was nothing subtle or nuanced about it. The school had to be overt in re-writing its future and our vision statement needed to match this.

For me, in my second headship, it was the first time I'd really thought about making the vision statement a living, breathing thing.

And the impact was transformational.

Your values

Next check your values align with your 'why'.

Vision and values are often referred to together, although they actually refer to two different, if connected, aspects of the school's core purpose.

Schools usually find the 'values' bit of the school's vision the most straightforward, but even here, there is often some confusion as to what a value is and what it is not. Brené Brown, in her fabulous book *Dare to Lead* (2018), explains the importance of values, stating that values-led organisations (such as schools) must '... *do more than profess our values, we practice them. We walk our talk—we are clear about what we believe and hold important, and we take care that our intentions, words, thoughts, and behaviours align with those beliefs.*'

We'll talk more about how to bring vision and values to life in the next chapter, but first we need to pin down what values are.

In an article in Forbes (2019), Michael Chavez concludes that values are meaningless unless they drive thinking and behaviours. He, like other writers in this sphere, add more depth to this notion by explaining that values should really be linked to core principles and actionable behaviours, such as in an article on the OKR Quickstart website (2025). For example, if one of our values is 'creativity' then our core principle is that children are provided with opportunities to think and act creatively, and this then drives behaviours that comes from this, e.g. creative thinking; children wanting to learn to play instruments, draw and dance, etc.

But bringing this back to the central role of values within a school setting, our school values should define what is most important to us as a school in terms of how we want people (ideally not just pupils, but parents and staff as well) to <u>think</u> and <u>behave</u>.

This should not be confused with simply defining 'good behaviour'; behaviours here refer to something much broader (such as the example of 'creative thinking' as a type of behaviour). Our school values also have to be both functional (achievable in the here and now) and aspirational (something which can be taught and developed over time).

Schools therefore need to spend time really defining what values matter most to them, and how they link to their core purpose – their 'why'.

And here, once again, less is more. It is simple for a school community to settle on a dozen values, but these will be impossible to remember, let alone actively teach on a daily basis. To be effective, schools need to narrow these down to no more than **four**, allowing them to truly become part of the daily conversation with pupils.

Making your school's mission part of the vision

The problem with vision statements is that they are, by their very definition, something which is just out of reach and describe a 'future state'. If done well, they will (in as short a sentence as possible) capture your school's 'why'.

What they will not do is capture the school's 'how'. And, as the Japanese proverb notes, '*Vision without action is a daydream*'. It is defining the 'how' – the school's core mission – which captures this action.

This is the next element of visioning where schools often lack clarity. Most schools don't do the next step and clearly define their 'how' – their mission – their 'active ingredients' for achieving the vision. This is because this next part seems to add more words, more complexity and (often) more confusion to the vision, so schools often leave this alone.

But by really pinning this down, it makes most other decisions regarding school improvement very simple: does this proposed initiative align with our vision and mission – yes or no?

Now, there are many clever people, who write many clever things on the subject of mission statements. I am not one of these people. However, there is a simple way to do this.

Once the simple (and short) vision statement (the 'why') has been clearly defined, we simply need to put the word 'by' after it and then list four (no more than this) key ingredients which the community believe are essential in meeting its vision.

I know what you're thinking: 'Simon, I've read loads of books on this and it is way more complicated than that!' And you may be right. However, I know from living, and seeing the impact of this process over the past 14 years, that it has truly defined how our school goes about school improvement.

For Blackhorse Primary, it looks like this:

We build champion learners (the vision, the 'why') through:

1. Extensive Opportunities

2. Expert Tuition

3. Purposeful Practice

4. Personal Effort

This is the mission… the 'how'.

Each active ingredient in our 'vision and mission statement' defines a core ingredient: four things which we as a school believe are fundamental in building champion learners. Sure, they need some elaboration to get their full meaning… but not much.

And I know that this approach is entirely replicable.

Having become Executive Headteacher of a second school just four minutes down the road from Blackhorse in 2022, we set about re-visioning, to make the school's long and proud history of inclusion marry up with our desire for greater aspiration and higher expectations of the children.

And so the school's vision and mission statement was written as follows:

At Emersons Green, we forge mighty futures by:

1. Pursuing Excellence
2. Building Bravery
3. Championing Uniqueness
4. Embracing Practice and Effort *(Well… it is the sister school of Blackhorse.)*

So what?

Well, at Blackhorse, where the vision and mission have been in place for some time, the statements above literally slap you in the face every time you turn a corner in the school (more on this in the next chapter). The four mission ingredients inform almost every decision regarding school improvement, from ensuring that our extra-curricular offer is the best in the area (extensive opportunities), to helping us decide that we needed a single teaching pedagogy across all subjects (expert tuition).

When we show parents around there is a simple story to tell. A story of where we came from, of the vision which we have for young people and how we will get them to become 'champion learners'.

And what of the impact on the school's reputation? Well, for nine consecutive years Blackhorse has been the second most over-subscribed school in the county. And also one of the most successful. We have achieved this by consistently and repeatedly articulating what we want for our children and how we will get there.

And as well as creating hundreds of metaphorical 'Champion Learners', we have also created more actual champion learners than any other school we know: 1 professional rugby player, 1 international 5000m runner and 18 national-level runners and athletes; plus scores of dancers, actors, singers, writers, mathematicians, engineers and artists. All who believe that they can and will succeed at life.

So, we do know that having a powerful (and simple, and short) vision works.

But I must now confess to the 'messiness'

I would love to end the chapter there… with Blackhorse giving itself a huge slap on the back and me sounding (vaguely) like I know what I'm talking about.

However, it would be remiss of the theme of the book if I didn't share the messiness which got us to our vision statement…

You see, I'd love to say that the school's vision to 'build champion learners' stemmed from a beautifully crafted visioning day where I, wisely and with dashing levels of insight, carried the school to a place where this compelling vision took flight.

But it didn't happen like that.

*

It was a hot May evening in 2011 and the staff were somewhat perturbed that yet another staff meeting was being taken up discussing the school's 'vision'. We'd just started working with a designer who was helping us change our old logo (which looked like a mafia threat) to something which matched our aspirations.

'So we're keeping the horse?' asked one staff member (the school name made the logo a clear steer – so, yes).

It was just a year before the London 2012 Olympics and we were already trying to use this national event as a vehicle to raise aspiration and (most urgently) standards.

'OK everyone,' says I, 'what do we think of when we think of horses?'

Cue lots of slightly unhelpful references to Black Beauty / Muffin the Mule / the donkey out of Shrek.

'Come on,' says I, trying not to sound irritated, 'something which captures our ambition, something which says we've changed as a school and that this is somewhere on the up.' (*Remembering that our SATs results were still amongst the lowest in the county and literally nobody wanted to send their children to Blackhorse.*)

And then the moment which led to the breakthrough…

'I have an idea!' came a voice in the corner of the room.

It was Nigel.

Possibly (despite being a lovely, lovely man) one of the most stubborn and, at times, openly rebellious members of staff, who had seen it all before and (from the look on his face) believed such frivolity to be (in the internal monologue I imagine for him) 'bollocks'.

I readied myself for some wise crack – and wasn't disappointed…

'How about "worth a punt"?' he quipped.

Cue hilarity from the staff.

'How about Champion Learners?' shot back Phil the Deputy…

And there it was. A gag played for laughs resulted in one of the most recognised school visions in our county.

Again, I'd love to tell you that this immediately led to our clearly defined mission ingredients.

But that would also be a lie.

The 'active ingredients' developed over the course of the next decade, as we worked out what it really meant to be a 'champion learner' at our school.

*

'Great,' you think. 'We too can have a snappy mission… if we wait around for a decade!'

But whilst it is true that this first iteration of the process took ten years, the second, at my second school, took just a matter of weeks. The school used its knowledge of itself; of its history and deeply held beliefs; and combined these to create a vision and mission which is already driving the work of the school and creating a simple narrative which parents can follow.

Key takeaways

1. Before you start crafting your school vision, you need to understand the school's 'origin story' and the core beliefs on which you wish to build a future for the school.

2. Spend time really defining your schools 'why', your USP.

3. Check that your values define the behaviours and thinking that you believe are most important to your school.

4. Write your vision statement in as few words as possible.

5. Define your 'how' by identifying four 'active ingredients' which are essential in achieving your vision.

Reflection tasks

Write the name of your school in the centre of a piece of paper. Without over-thinking it, around it write all the reasons that your school exists. Take 'teaching the National Curriculum' for a given – look for what makes your school different and special. How closely is this reflected in your current vision statement?

_____

_____

_____

_____

_____

Complete the table below, showing how your values translate into observable pupil behaviours,.

Value	Behaviours which you'd see around school to demonstrate this value

Do a quick poll with your staff/ governors. How many of them can recite the school's vision statement word for word? How many have the gist of it? How many have no idea?

_____

_____

_____

_____

_____

List all the school improvement actions, in the past year, which have been directly influenced by the school's vision.

_____
_____
_____
_____
_____

What will you do next to make your vision statement more accessible and relevant to the life of the school?

_____
_____
_____
_____
_____

Chapter 3

The importance of symbols and rituals

The stories we tell ourselves

The place was like a swanky golf club.

Not like any school I'd worked in.

Not like any school I knew.

As you walked up the path to the entrance, lined by perfectly manicured flowerbeds, signs declared your arrival at the school. Across the threshold you were greeted by an immaculate lobby, with the school's mission and vision emblazoned across the door lintel. Beyond that, you entered the school proper, and, before I'd taken ten steps into the place I knew exactly what the school was about.

The gleaming trophy cabinet; the beautifully mounted work on display; the sofas where children idly strummed guitars. The mission which this school was fixated on was in no doubt…

I'd been a Head for about a month and I desperately needed a golden bullet to lift my school out of the mire.

But how do you improve a school which seems so crestfallen?

I cast around for ideas and happened upon a newspaper article about Waycroft Primary, a school in Bristol which had recently (back in 2007) been judged Outstanding in all 27 inspection areas. Indeed, the lead inspector said it was the best school they'd ever seen, not bothering to give them any areas for development – because they concluded that they couldn't find any.

After touring his stunning school, I eventually sat down with the then headteacher Simon Rowe (now Senior HMI), and asked him what I should do to reverse my school's fortunes.

'Sort out the environment; sort out behaviour; sort out teaching,' he shot back, without a moment's hesitation, 'in that exact order…and oh… read this…'

He pressed into my hand a pamphlet written by the late, great Sir Tim Brighouse entitled *Essential Pieces – the jigsaw of an essential school*.

Both his advice, and the pamphlet he thrust into my hand, have been my blueprint for school improvement ever since.

*

The stories we tell ourselves – the importance of symbols and rituals

Much of my personal philosophy of education harks back to a quote from 2500 years ago…

> 'Excellence is an art won by training and habituation. We do not act rightly because we have virtue or excellence, but we rather have those because we have acted rightly.
>
> We are what we repeatedly do.
>
> Excellence, then, is not an act but a habit.'
>
> Aristotle

Or as Doug Lemov notes in the brilliant *Teach like a Champion*: 'We change from the outside in.'

Once we accept that we are governed (either consciously or sub-consciously) by teachable and learnable habits, then symbols, rituals and, above all, routines, become the invisible teacher, constantly reinforcing what it is to belong to this particular school tribe.

We'll explore more explicitly the impact of routines on behaviour later on, but first, we need to understand the symbolism and ritualised behaviours which our schools, again either through omission or commission, espouse.

Pick your symbols and rituals – or others will do this for you

Symbolism and ritualism is as old as human civilisation. It has how we reinforce the bonds of the tribe.

But it is often something which we don't explicitly seek to influence.

All schools have symbols and rituals, but not all schools have explicitly chosen these to serve a clear purpose. Most often they have simply developed organically over time, often informed by some sense of vision but not often explicitly led by it.

Worse still, when there has been no consideration of what symbols and rituals matter within a school then sometimes another tribe, led by unruly students, or sometimes even unruly staff, establish their own symbols and rituals which may seek to actually undermine the school's core mission. How often have we seen a culture take hold on the playground or dining hall (or staffroom!) when no stronger rituals have been established?

Sure, there has been a move of late to be more explicit in teaching classroom routines (the rituals of learning), but how many schools consider which routines are taught to explicitly reinforce the school's vision?

Once we have agreed on a compelling vision, mission and values for our school, I believe that we must then operationalise this, oft invisible, core purpose by the symbols and rituals which we choose to wrap around it.

So choose which symbols and rituals reinforce your vision and values carefully – or others will do it for you.

A tidy school is a good school

I have visited a great many schools over the last twenty years: a few which are genuinely excellent; most which are thoroughly good; and a few which are in deep trouble.

And there is one universal truth: I have never visited an excellent school which is untidy.

Ron Berger, in his book *An Ethic of Excellence* (2003), which is so brilliantly summarised in Sonia Thompson's *An Ethic of Excellence in Action* (2022), describes this universal truth perfectly:

> *'A clean and well-kept building guarantees nothing about the quality of work children will accomplish within it. But it matters. It's a message. It's a visual model of the ethic within the building. The building doesn't have to be a palace… but it has to show the children, the teachers and the parents that somebody cares about them.'*

And so when I'm mentoring a new headteacher in a school in difficulty, my first advice is always the same: get a skip.

As is my second piece of advice: get another skip.

Indeed, by the end of my first term as the new headteacher in my struggling school, we'd managed to fill seventeen skips.

Both a tidy school and an untidy school serve as a powerful visual metaphor for everyone within it.

Your vision, values and mission

Your vision, values and mission should hit any visitor across the face the moment they step through the front door.

You have one opportunity to make the right impression, whether that be to visiting parents, professionals or, most importantly, the children. A visitor to your school will make a subconscious judgement about what you are about within ten seconds of entering the building.

So think carefully about this one chance.

The driveway and path to the school's front door is where the first impressions form, so at Blackhorse Primary visitors are greeted by four enormous banners adorned with giant photos, each proclaiming one of the four 'active ingredients' within our mission statement. Through the fence, the grounds are on full show, with a 5m wooden finger sign pointing to 'Blackhorse Farm', 'The Castaway Camp', 'Blackhorse Cove' and a dozen other places.

Above the door reads the words 'Welcome to Blackhorse Primary School – we build champion learners'. And beyond that, as you enter the school proper, you are greeted by the best displays we can muster, followed by a floor to ceiling infographic of the school's mission. Then framed photos of all the alumni who have become professional athletes, musicians and actors (currently five in the last decade). Then the gleaming trophy cabinets. Then the wing-backed chairs of the 'reading room'.

Before you have taken ten steps into our school – you know what we are about. And whilst it is a deliberately overpowering visual message for visitors, it symbolises to every child and staff member, who walk past it every single day, that they are the champions who we are in the business of building.

When some of the school council were showing around a parent, they described this area as 'the corridor of pride' – a made-up (but fabulous) description all of their own.

Give your values character

In 2011, we happened upon a silly little idea which has possibly had more impact on children internalising our school's values than any other. We invented a gang of superheroes unique to Blackhorse, whom we would use to teach the children what the values meant in practice.

They were a gang of five (initially badly drawn, then in 2015 professionally rendered) characters used to tell the story of what we value:

- Brave Bear – a bear who really isn't very brave, but is trying.
- Samda the Successful – a girl whose superpower is nothing other than personal effort every single day.
- Respect the Wonder Dog – a level-headed artist who knows he must earn respect.
- Proud Pony – who loves football and her family's connection with the St Kitts Cricket team. Never follows the crowd.
- And finally… 'Captain Champion' – trying (and often failing) to be a superhero – but God loves a trier!

BLACKHORSE PRIMARY SCHOOL

Every assembly started with a story about the characters. The rewards are built around them.

We repeated the same exercise recently at my other school, Emersons Green, with exactly the same impact to highlight its USP (a small 1-form entry school surrounded by large ones which needed to feel more powerful) as a virtue by creating a band of mice who live in the skirting boards but believe they are lions (fitting the school's strap line 'forging mighty futures'), complete with tiny doors which appeared in the aforementioned skirting boards which the staff claim to know nothing about. And where, outside, the children promptly started leaving tiny letters about how they'd been mighty today... and the occasional chunk of cheese sandwich...

It sounds a ridiculous frivolity – but the hidden meaning isn't lost on the children: they *are* 'Captain Champion' – flawed yet wildly optimistic ... they *are* 'Emerson Mouse' – small yet mighty!

So if you want your values to fly – give them a superhero cloak!

The power of mantras

Again, faffing about with pithy slogans might again seem like a silly waste of time with a million and one serious pedagogical decisions to make. But, again, discretionary effort comes more from feeling than cold logic. And how people *feel* about the school's vision and the journey you and they are embarked upon has as much impact as the practical, sensible, logical things which you as leader are doing to improve the school. A clearly articulated vision will allow your team to coalesce around the school's core mission, but it will be pithy mantras which keep that mission at the forefront of people's minds.

As previously discussed, a well-written school slogan should capture the entire essence of the school in no more than five words. This can then become a mantra – a constant 'call to arms' for children and staff alike. Since the re-visioning exercise at Emersons Green Primary school in 2022, where we decided to 'Forge Mighty Futures', the staff mention the idea of 'might' in as many interactions with the children as possible. The PE kit has the word 'Mighty' emblazoned on the back.

The result? Children *feel* more… well… mighty! They strive for betterment and reject mediocracy in their learning in a manner which is tangible. They talk openly of being mighty… of *wanting* to be mighty. Parents, sceptical at first, are seeing the benefit of an explicitly positive mantra.

Indeed, the wider community also notices, and when a friend told their seven-year-old child that they were working in Emersons Green the following day, her daughter noted 'That's the mighty school, isn't it?'.

Oh, and SATs results have gone from average to excellent.

Tell stories and create legends

In Steven Bartlett's excellent book *The Diary of a CEO* (2023), he describes the best companies as behaving like cults. In his 'ten steps to build company culture' he notes that leaders should '*Use myths, stories, [school] specific vocabulary and legends, along with symbols and habits, to reinforce the [school] culture and embed it into the collective consciousness.*'

In the booklet that so influenced me almost twenty years ago, Tim Brighouse knew it too, arguing that good storytelling was at the heart of manifesting a school's vision and mission on a day to day basis.

As teachers at heart, school leaders are usually pretty good at telling stories. But I rarely see schools harnessing this powerful (and completely free) psychological tool. Instead, most schools give up this advantage in the name of modesty. Instead, we need to be constantly telling stories about victories, big and small, past and present; about ex-students who went on to do great things; about the impact of this or that initiative; about the hundreds of tiny wins celebrated by individual pupils on a daily basis. And we must tell these stories by linking them back to the school's mission; as evidence of its power and success.

These stories. These legends. These myths. They matter.

They bind both the community to the school's declared mission and seep into the children's collective memory.

Here's an example from the excellent Sonia Thompson, who describes how stories are the beating heart of her school's success.

Case Study: Sonia Thompson

Headteacher of St Matthews Primary, Birmingham, Director of St Matthew's Research School, author of *The Ethics of Excellence in Action*

Why do the stories we tell ourselves matter?

Stories matter at St Matthew's Primary School. The ones in books matter immensely (we are a school that adores reading) and the ones we tell ourselves about our school and what we want to achieve matter. The stories we tell ourselves have an ambitious plot. Stories where our curriculum, values and mission statement communicate to our children, families and teachers that we are unflinching about the business of education and social justice. These are our daily read-alouds. They are the stories of our school culture.

When we composed our mission statement, all of our school community was involved, and our brief was simple: to succinctly capture the story of our ambition for our children and for each other. We wanted our story to have longevity. A story that we could retell and continuously add to. It had to be a story that we would be proud of, in order to hold ourselves accountable to its challenge; to always do our utmost for our children in order for them not only to thrive but also to flourish.

The consistency of our story has been and is key for us. As a school in Nechells, one of the most deprived areas in Birmingham (and in the UK), we are all too aware of the acute distractions and challenges. These narratives are often more dramatic and unflinching. Stories of poverty, unemployment and crime. There are also preconceived and negative stories from some sections of society, about children and families from our area. This can often engender perceptions of what our children can or cannot achieve. We wanted our school story to demonstrate just how wrong these perceptions are!

My own story echoes the stories of the school I currently serve. I am a child from a large family – six brothers and three sisters – born and raised in a highly disadvantaged area, in inner city Birmingham. My Jamaican parents wanted the best for all their children and their own story of survival, in communities that were not always welcoming, instilled a sense of determination and grit in us all. They would not let other people tell their children's stories, or determine our future.

My parents' story, particularly the joy and despair (when the finances were tight), of raising ten children to value education, in an education system that was often hostile to black and brown students, became my story. As I became a teacher, a leader, who then moved into headship, I was conscious of my mission. To counteract the platitudinous statements about 'children like me, from areas like mine'. Instead, I battled to ensure that my students' stories (and outcomes) exemplify my relentless and unflinching determination for them to succeed.

The symbols and ritual of our story

To enable continuous success to happen at St Matthew's, it has always been about being deliberate and intentional with our symbols and rituals. These include evidence-informed practice, tight behaviour and learning systems and as a church school prayer and spirituality. One of our key symbols is CAP – courage, attainment and pride. This value symbolises our commitment to an 'ethic of excellence'. The ritual of physically putting on our imaginary 'CAPs' everyday, tells a beautiful story. It is a story that 'wearing your CAP with dignity' – 'Gere piliem cum dignate' - will empower you to not only learn more and remember more but also to do it with increasing confidence. Our children understand that we want the best for them and this symbol and ritual encapsulates a way of achieving that best. It is their story and our symbols and rituals help them to write it.

Their stories

We have enabled our children to live their stories through our ethos. When visitors come to St Matthew's they say they can feel that our children 'want to learn and they love to learn'. Their eagerness to learn more challenging stuff is infectious and drives our determination to do whatever we can to realise this.

From what our data is telling us, and as importantly for us, the positive comments from our students and families, it seems that we are beginning to redress the equity imbalance, which often blurs the learning lines when working in an area of high disadvantage. The stories that matter to us at St Matthew's, with their ambitious plots of social justice and commitment, are being written, read and retold. With each retelling, the stories that matter have become more powerful, more motivating and more embedded within our school culture. That matters the most.

Yet again, whilst stories and rituals may appear 'a nothing' at first glance, Sonia demonstrates that often they are the key to everything.

Sing from the rooftops what you're about (literally)

Community schools have much to learn here from faith schools.

You visit any good faith school and you will quickly notice that they have imported century-old worship practices into framing the school's core purpose (often employing quotes from scripture). Often the school will have a particular hymn which embodies its mission and often they will use the daily prayer to remind the children of the values which are held most dear.

Look at the independent sector, particularly older schools with hundreds of years of heritage, and you will notice that they also are adept at harnessing this power of collective worship to further the school's own values.

Having been a Head of a church school, I 'borrowed' some of these practices in my next headship. I figured that if I have to legally say a prayer at the end of every assembly, then (much like a traditional church service) it would be a school prayer which we chant at the end of every assembly – a visible reminder of the people we want to be.

Likewise, a school song is another great way to hammer home the message that we are a single tribe and have common values and goals.

Be 'that' headteacher

I got my first leadership role as Key Stage 2 Leader at Wheatfield Primary School, a brand new school on a brand new estate, led by the irrepressible Christine Dursley – a headteacher who utterly believed that Wheatfield was exceptional. She told this to pretty much everyone who came near the school: to parents, to the children (constantly), to the staff and to any LA or Ofsted bod who came a knocking.

As a result, she gained a somewhat partisan reputation amongst the other heads who sometimes felt that her 'masters of the universe' school mantra was 'a bit much'.

But, as a staff, we loved her for it.

She made us believe that all the extra work we chose to do served some higher purpose and edged us to greatness. The pithy mantras seeped deep into our subconscious and she was their champion.

At my leaving do in 2003 I drunkenly promised her that I'd 'make the whole world Wheatfield'.

In many ways, my past and current schools are a testament to this influence. Be that headteacher.

Finally, take all of the staples out of the display boards

'What…?' repeated the Chair of Governors, looking both simultaneously confused and offended at the suggestion, '…all of them??'

'I'm afraid so… all of them.'

There was a cold silence.

'But it'll take hours,' she protested.

I handed her the staple remover and she and I spent several hours removing twenty years of staples from the tatty and unloved display boards which had previously displayed tatty and unloved work.

Was this the best use of a headteacher's and chair of governor's time? Possibly not. But in those hours we were passed by pretty much every member of staff. They saw that the headteacher and chair of governors meant it when they said that displays were a metaphor for how we felt about our school.

Within a month the displays across the school were beautiful.

Key takeaways

- A good school is a tidy school. If your school is not a tidy school, get a skip… and then another, until it is.
- Pick your symbols and rituals – they promote behaviours and attitudes.
- Your vision should metaphorically grab visitors by the lapels as they walk through the school.
- Mantras matter – know what your school's mantra is.
- Create legends: stories of the school's success.

Reflection tasks

Stand at the entrance of your school, right by the road where parents and visitors first step foot onto your site. Now walk down the drive, into the lobby and then into the school. Note down all the things you see (big and small) which illustrate and support your school's vision and mission, or which undermine it. How clearly would a visitor walking this walk know what your school is about by the time they have spent ten seconds inside the building?

_____
_____
_____
_____
_____

What is your school's mantra? What slogans are used by adults (and children) around the school as a shorthand for your vision and mission?

_____
_____
_____
_____
_____

List which rituals and symbols your school has – in assembly, in daily routines, in reward systems – which promote the school's vision and mission?

_____
_____
_____
_____
_____

Re-read the last ten newsletters to parents. How often is the school's vision and mission promoted within these, through stories which exemplify it in action?

_____
_____
_____
_____
_____

Over the course of a week, listen for how many times staff, especially senior staff, relate achievements or aims back to the school's vision and mission in conversation with others.

_____
_____
_____
_____
_____

Chapter 4
Improving behaviour

Give a little respect

'You'll be needing this,' snapped the stocky Lead Lunch Break Supervisor, thrusting a walkie-talkie into my hand. It was my first meeting with the formidable Mrs Smythe, a 'no nonsense' type of person, who'd worked at the school as long as anyone could remember.

'Oh… thank you…' I replied, examining the item curiously.

'It's so's we can contact you…' she remarked sternly, '…for the fights.'

'The fights..?'

'The fights… Lots of 'em… We'll call you on this when they happen.'

And with that she left.

I had already started to notice that behaviour at the school was 'problematic' before completing my first day (what with children trying to burn down the school and telling me to 'fuck off' in assembly and all) but this seemed even more confusing.

Surely I didn't need a walkie-talkie to be summoned to deal with fights? I'd been a deputy at a quaint village school in a quaint market town. Fighting in the playground, beyond the usual pushing and shoving over football, was unheard of. Surely, children fighting in the playground wasn't common for 'city folk'?

'FIGHT!!!' the screech came over the walkie-talkie (which I henceforth dubbed my 'fight-phone').

I leapt from my office chair and headed to the playground.

Give a little respect – how to improve behaviour

Behaviour in schools is one of the first areas any new headteacher should turn their attention to. Nothing will undo your best efforts to improve a school quicker than ineffective behaviour management and children running riot. We may not be the ones stood in front of 30 children every day 'doing' the behaviour management at a micro level, but at a macro level we make the weather.

Remember the sage-like advice from the ever-wise Simon Rowe, when asked how to improve a school:

1. Sort the environment.
2. Sort behaviour.
3. Sort teaching and learning.

In some schools you may just be looking to make minor improvements to specific areas. In others, like in my first headship, there may need to be a radical change in culture.

So, unless behaviour at your school is absolutely perfect, it should be an area which school leaders constantly return to.

Remember – the headteacher makes the weather!

As head, you decide what the behavioural culture will be like within your school. This should be a fairly uncontroversial statement, yet I still come across many heads who feel that they have little influence in improving behaviour and attitudes. And whilst we cannot fully control the behaviour of pupils entirely – they are sentient beings who will do a whole host of things for a whole host of reasons – we can (and must) be the person who 'sets the weather' within a school by articulating and then defending our expectations regarding pupil behaviour. Only the headteacher, and their senior team, has the decision-making authority to set and sustain a whole-school behaviour approach, so it is wise to ask yourself what sort of behaviour culture you wish to enact (and why). As, whilst you'd imagine that there would be a single, deeply researched and evidence-led, behaviour pedagogy… there isn't.

Ideology or science?

Understand that behaviour management approaches come as much from ideology as science.

You'd imagine that pupil behaviour, with its ability to make or break a pupil's life-chances, as well as determine how successful a school is at educating pupils, would be the subject of centuries of scientific enquiry, resulting in balanced and carefully evidenced approaches universally adopted by teachers and leaders across the globe.

Sadly this isn't the case.

Like so many areas of education, behaviour management approaches are often deeply partisan and ideological.

Let me explain…

In the 'progs' corner we have Paul Dix and his excellent book *When the Adults Change, Everything Changes* (2017). I read his book and found it very useful. Sadly, upon hearing that I've read and liked his book, one pedagogical tribe will tut, mutter something about me being a 'woke Guardian-reading liberatti', possibly 'a communist', and almost certainly 'an enemy of promise'. And promptly stop reading this book and go write something pithy on social media.

In the 'trads' corner we have Tom Bennett and his excellent book *Running the Room* (2020). I read his book and found it very useful. Sadly, upon hearing that I've read and liked his book, another pedagogical tribe will tut, mumble something about me being a 'Daily Mail-reading Tory', and almost certainly a 'child-hating edu-fascist'. And promptly stop reading this book and go write something pithy on social media.

This is the nonsense which surrounds this all-important aspect of school development.

My advice? Read both books (and also the excellent EEF research papers on the subject). And be very wary of seeking ideologies which simply confirm your own biases. As a rule of thumb, any edu-commentator promoting their behaviour approach with absolute certainty of its efficacy (whilst rubbishing all other approaches) will almost certainly be talking bollocks.

Culture and belonging

Culture and belonging determine how we all behave. So create the best gang!

In *Running the Room*, Tom Bennett writes about the importance of Durkheim's 'social identity theory'. In short, it's our basic human need to be part of a gang. Preferably the most powerful gang. It's a simple evolutionary advantage – and a fact not lost on even primary-aged children.

The young chap who greeted my request to walk into assembly on my first day of headship knew it. As did all his peers.

In a dysfunctional school, counter-culture is the most powerful gang. Misbehaving is what the tribe do. Learning isn't what the tribe engages in.

Whilst this is an extreme example, we all know it to be true. Once the majority have decided what the behavioural norms are, for better or worse, most children will either overtly or covertly fall into line. This is why it's difficult to change an entrenched culture of misbehaviour, whilst relatively simple to sustain a positive behaviour culture. Group behaviours self-sustain.

If you're looking to change 'the way we've always done it here' – whether that be walking into the hall quietly or not shouting out in class – the majority will resist this attack on the group norm. Leaders then need to overwhelm this negative prevalent behaviour code with what I'd (only half-jokingly) describe as a totalitarian regime: strict enforcement and indoctrination in a new world view. It can take years to do this – but every school fights this fight as it speaks to the heart and soul of the community.

And, as we've discussed in earlier chapters, culture is the outcome of a strong vision and ethos.

Just as we all long to be part of a powerful gang, as humans, our brains make sense of the world by learning stories about the world told to us by others. This is the most common route to cultural understanding. Then, having internalised these stories, we make up stories of our own which confirm this biased narrative of the world around us – our internal monologue which we use to rationalise the chaotic by shaping it into a world view.

As we discussed in previous chapters, these stories will either be written into mythology by the school, or (in the absence of this) will be made up by individuals and groups all by themselves.

Whilst we all know this to be true in our schools, surprisingly little effort is put into ensuring that the children in our care feel like they belong; like they are cared for by a gang which has their best interests at heart. They should feel this connection at home (although sadly not always) and through the other communities which they belong to (although sadly not always). But do we as schools really think hard about how we will foster this sense of belonging?

As mentioned earlier, this tribal connection is built using the symbols and rituals which we weave into children's everyday experiences. However, it is also built through deliberate opportunities to bring individuals together and giving them a sense of common purpose. Some of the best class teachers I know foster this sense of tribe (more on this later), but we can also achieve this through organised opportunities to reinforce belonging.

At my current schools, we noticed that children who belonged to one of the school's numerous extra-curricular clubs, tended to attend school more and behave better. Those who had a special T-shirt to wear on club days, better again. They had a physical, and, to them, slightly exclusive signifier of belonging. And who doesn't love a special T-shirt! Add in internal myths and legends linked directly to these internal clubs, and these children felt an overwhelming feeling of tribal connection. Conversely, we also noticed that children who didn't attend extra-curricular activities appeared to feel less loyalty and connection towards the school and their peers, resulting in lower attendance, lower attainment and more problematic behaviours.

Explicitly teach the behaviour you expect to see

Again, this is no great epiphany – a teacher a hundred years ago would know this.

Both Paul Dix and Tom Bennett make this a central plank of their writing. And yet, there are many voices in the world of education (most of them on social media) who think that teaching children how to behave is somehow akin to indoctrination by an authoritarian state. Indeed, since Covid, I believe that we as a society have lost our way a bit on this one. Families seem confused by an explosion of parenting approaches which espouse children being allowed to decide for themselves whether to go to bed on time, eat their greens or play in traffic. I fear that, as a society, we are often now expecting children to learn how to regulate their behaviours, without instructing them how to do this, and providing appropriate boundaries to ensure that they feel safe.

In Doug Lemov's *Teach Like a Champion*, he notes that one of the greatest failings of a teacher or school is in assuming that children will naturally know the 'right' way to behave. We cannot simply expect children to hold the same values regarding behavioural norms as we do. Some will – mainly because their life experiences will have been similar to our own (and we will quickly decide that these children are 'nice'). Other children simply won't know what the behaviours we are asking for look like (and we run the risk of quickly deciding that these children are just 'naughty').

Both Paul and Tom make the point that when a teacher asks 'Would you do that at home?' they assume all homes are the same. And they aren't. So we must be explicit with all the behaviours which we want children to display.

So if we want children to know how to behave, we must devote classroom time to teaching them. And this is where 90% of good behaviour management comes down to routines.

Routines are a teacher's best friend

Again, whilst we may not as school leaders be the ones designing and implementing the minutiae of classroom routines, we are the people who should set the expectations that routines exist. We are also the people who need to then constantly check that routines are being followed in every class, every day.

The importance of routines are almost universally accepted as one of the essential foundations that learning behaviours are built upon.

In the classroom, this means the teacher turning every expectation into a three-step process. Instead of just expecting the children to know how to sit on the carpet, we must explicitly teach them the steps to be successful:

1. Find your carpet square.

2. Sit with your hands in your lap.

3. Look at the teacher.

Whilst some may think this a bit OTT (and each school must decide for themselves the level of formality which best matches their ethos and values), the principle is sound and will benefit the most vulnerable children most. For example, if you live in a house in which you are used to sitting for extended periods and giving an adult full attention, then you will probably arrive at school already having learnt how to sit and listen to a teacher. However, if you live in an overcrowded house where this isn't your norm, this will seem extremely alien. Again, this isn't rocket science – and any Early Years teacher instinctively knows to do this – but often as the children get older we forget this need for explicit routines as we assume that the children should 'just know how to do it by now'. Just because a pupil is 14, doesn't mean they know what your expectations are (although they may be less easily incentivised by the chance of a gold sticker)!

When it comes to how the children interact in the wider school, leaders and teachers need to again reach a consensus on how basic things should be done. Just as every child's home may not be the same, every member of staff's understanding of how children should walk down the corridor may also not be the same, and so routines which affect everyone need agreeing centrally.

Constantly call out good behaviour

Both Paul and Tom note that good teachers make 'good behaviour' easy, and 'bad behaviour' hard – something which requires effort.

Paul Dix talks about 'catching the children behaving well'. Often we take good behaviours for granted and only highlight poor behaviours. Yet, by constantly calling out good behaviours, we are providing models and reference points as to what those good behaviours look like in everyday situations.

Again, an ECT will be taught this in their first weeks of teacher training, yet in many schools there is no consistent and agreed approach for systematically highlighting positive behaviour. We all know that the purpose of calling out good behaviour publicly is to both reinforce to the individual that they have made a good choice (which they will then seek to replicate) and to the class as a whole class, so that they will seek to replicate this behaviour as well. However, the most successful schools have this systematic 'naming and praising' of good behaviour codified in systems which are clearly outlined within the behaviour policy. In these schools, the adults explicitly identify the positive behaviour which they have observed, using agreed language, and then provide a range of appropriate rewards which tell both the individual and their peers that this positive behaviour is highly valued.

Whilst tokens or house points or dojos can be useful, we need to avoid creating token economies which, may be easy to monitor, but quickly become devoid of meaning for the child. For example, I remember receiving a text from my son's secondary school noting that 'Archie has received +2 behaviour points today'. Telling parents about positive behaviour which has been observed is one reward which children value the most. However, when they become numbers, devoid of context or meaning, they become a token economy. Worst still, inflation quickly occurs in such economies with teachers giving uneven amounts of rewards for different levels of effort.

Certainty of sanction is more effective than weight of sanction

Now this is the arena in which the Edu-culture-wars are typically fought...

On the one side are the 'lock 'em in a cage if they look out of the window' brigade. They confidently declare that harsh punitive punishment is what gets results and that 'Tom Bennett told them to' (he didn't). On the other side are the 'give them a hot chocolate if they set fire to the hamster' brigade. They don't believe in sanctions at all and believe that a singalong with an acoustic guitar is how to deal with an unruly class. They firmly believe that Paul Dix told them this (he didn't).

This 'pick a side' narrative is not just exhausting, but also dangerous. It allows loud voices to on social media to grandstand and drives bad, or more often misunderstood, approaches to behaviour management. As Dylan Wiliam says *'Everything works somewhere, nothing works everywhere'*.

During my time as a LA behaviour consultant, I discovered that in many local secondary schools, the number of suspensions and permanent exclusions had doubled every year for the past five years. The reason? Fatal mutation. Schools had heard of schools in other parts of the country using 'Ready to Learn' detention booths to improve behaviour and rushed in the same policy, without creating a coherent behaviour strategy which married a strong culture and positive reinforcement with any sanctions. As a result, children were being turfed out of lessons for increasingly minor infringements and the 'Ready to Learn' rooms filled up and became learning institutions in their own right – with pupils learning how to behave badly. So the schools put in place increasingly harsh sanctions for any pupil messing about in 'Ready to Learn' and, hey presto, exclusions skyrocketed.

On the other side of the coin, I ran a successful 'Better Behaviours' project across the county which focused on creating a behaviour culture in schools. It included the need for appropriate sanctions but, in some schools, staff misunderstood the message and stopped using sanctions altogether. This was never given as a message and, again, was the result of fatal mutation. The result in these schools was equally as disastrous, with children's poor behaviour choices going unchecked.

Sanctions have been, and always will be, necessary. Children need boundaries to thrive and feel safe. It is how we apply these boundaries and sanctions which makes the difference.

Paul Dix talks about staff never being forced to 'busk it' when it comes to sanctions. Tom Bennett talks about 'certainty rather than severity'. The inevitability of a sanction sends out a powerful message that poor behaviours will always be challenged and school rules enforced. This is often obvious with obvious or serious behaviour breaches, but can sometimes become more fluid when it comes to pushing the boundaries on the small stuff (which can quickly become the big stuff).

Again, schools must decide for themselves how to respond to low level disruptive behaviours. I for one am not a fan of heavy sanctions for forgetting a pen, but I do think that if 'being ready' is one of the school rules (as it is at my school) then a 1 minute conversation at the start of breaktime about why not having equipment causes problems is probably appropriate. What is important is that the school has an agreed approach which links directly to the school rules and the routines which we mentioned earlier. The rules must be easy for everyone to remember – ours are simply: *Be Ready, Be Respectful, Be Safe.* Once agreed, the sanctions need to be applied consistently.

Respect

You and the whole staff need to like and respect the children unconditionally.

'I just need to pop and see Kane.'

It was the middle of August and we were only supposed to be dropping into the school where my wife teaches Year 3 for a couple of minutes. Kane was a child she had taught the previous year who was spending his summer at the school's holiday club. He had come into the class with a reputation as having a violent temper which could result in a plethora of 'deregulated behaviours'.

The first thing Julie told him the previous September was that she would always be there for him and would 'have his back'. The second thing she told him was that there were rules in her classroom, and no matter how bad a day he was having, she cared for him enough to ensure that he followed her rules. In so doing she created a relationship based on deep care *and* high expectations. After a year in her class there were still occasional outbursts – but they were occasional.

'Hi Kane,' called Julie across the busy holiday club hall.

Kane ran over and gave her an enormous hug before Julie introduced me to him. 'This is Kane who I've told you all about. He's a great pupil!'

It was a nothing.

Ten minutes out of our otherwise un-busy day. But to Kane it spoke volumes: 'My teacher who has showed unconditional positive regard for me all year has taken time out of her holiday to check in on me. To underline that she really does care. I matter to her.'

*

A thousand teachers will show the same level of unconditional positive regard in a thousand tiny ways every day. In so doing they will steer a thousand children towards better behavioural interactions and a brighter future.

But, again, in our schools, is this something we leave to the personality and experience of individual teachers? Or do we include an expectation of unconditional positive regard within our behaviour policies?

Manage complex behaviours proportionately

As illustrated in the story above, it is essential that any school behaviour culture is a mix of both deep personal care for the child *and* high expectations of their behaviour and conduct.

However, in a complex world where children sometimes have challenging lives (which sometimes translate into challenging behaviours) I have seen individual teachers, and sometimes whole schools, fall into the trap of pitying children to the point where any and all inappropriate behaviours go without sanction. The result? The child learns that there are no secure boundaries. The behaviours persist and deepen. Their existing disadvantage (either as a result of circumstance or additional need) is in no way lessened, but their chance of succeeding in education is fatally compromised. They either eventually meet with a different behaviour code in 'big school' and are quickly expelled, or, in the name of inclusion, teachers lower their academic expectations to the point where the child's education never recovers.

We know more about special needs and disabilities now than at any point in history. We know that neurodiversity, ADHD and speech and language difficulties are often present when children struggle to navigate the behavioural norms schools seek to impose. A good school will be adept at making sensible adaptations to behaviour approaches which take account of these additional needs. For example, a child with a profile of needs-led behaviours should have their own behaviour plan outlining exactly how they should be supported in class and what rewards and sanctions will be applied. These plans will seek to modify behaviour over time and that may mean that staff manage behaviours differently than for the majority of children.

However, irrespective of need, children need to learn that behaviours have consequences. As Paul Dix puts it: 'As an adult, you won't be able to wave your EHCP at the magistrate and expect clemency'. However, I have seen some schools lose themselves when they try and accommodate any and all behaviours in the name of inclusion.

My schools have the highest number of children with EHCPs in the county. Most of these are for Speech, Language and Communication. But if you are violent towards a member of staff, then you are going home. It doesn't matter what your needs are, this is an absolute rule – an automatic suspension for the remainder of the day. We do this because we believe that all children need to learn that they can't harm others. And, over time, we can demonstrate that it does result in such behaviours reducing. I know of other schools that have a 'no exclusions' rule and this is a decision which each school must take for themselves.

A number of years ago I visited a school in Leeds which had a truly transformational approach towards behaviour (and some of the best academic results in the country). Chris Dyson, the Headteacher of Parklands at the time, explains more…

Case Study: Chris Dyson

Deputy CEO of Create Trust, and former headteacher at Parklands Primary School Leeds (at the time one of the highest achieving schools in England)

Hey, everyone! Grab a cuppa or a nice cup of hot chocolate (in a Paul Dix #WhenTheAdultsChange mug if possible), and let's dive into the chapter about 'Improving Behaviour'. Picture yourself on a chilly Monday morning at Parklands Primary School; it's a day that sticks with me for more reasons than one. It's the story about a little lad named Stewie and how we turned things around with just a sprinkle of respect and a whole lotta love.

So, there I was, standing at the school gates, greeting every child by name – one of the best parts of my job. The first five minutes can set the tone for the rest of the day, after all. And let me tell ya, when you're a headteacher, you quickly become a human thermometer gauging the temperature of the whole school.

Now, Stewie, he's a sparky one – five foot nothing and full of beans, but on this particular morning, he was as grumpy as a bear woken up early from hibernation. You couldn't miss it; it was almost like he had a thunder cloud floating over his head. He stomped through the gates, kicking a stray pebble like it owed him money narrowly missing several staff cars.

'Morning, Stewie! Everything alright, mate?' I called out, flashing my best 'I've got your back' smile.

'Nothin',' he grunted, not even looking up. Boy, was I not convinced, but I knew better than to push it right then.

I made a mental note and carried on saying my hellos, but Stewie was already on my radar. Over the next couple of hours, reports filtered in: Stewie refused to do his work, Stewie had an argument with another student – classic signs something was up. By lunchtime, it was clear. I had to step in before things really snowballed.

So I caught up with Stewie in the corridor, post-lunch and pre-afternoon lessons – prime time for a little heart-to-heart.

'Stewie, how about we take a walk?' I suggested, putting my arm lightly around his shoulder. That corridor felt like the longest stretch of land in Yorkshire, but it's our own little private space for these crucial chats.

At first, he was resistant, stiff as a board. Kids pick up on genuine concern like you wouldn't believe, and eventually, he started to soften. We found ourselves outside on the playground benches, his favourite spot. He drew shapes in the dirt with his shoe, avoiding eye contact.

'You wanna tell me what's going on, buddy?'

For what felt like ages, he didn't speak. But sometimes, silence is the best part of a conversation. Finally, he muttered, 'My mum lost her job, and we don't have money for heating, we can't put money in the 'lecky box so I have no clean jumper, and mum went without tea last night.' It all came out!

Boom. Just like that, it hit you right in the gut. These kids carry the weight of the world on their little shoulders. The classroom was the last thing on his mind; survival and worry had taken front seat.

I took a deep breath, trying to push down the lump in my throat. 'Mate, I had no idea. That's a heavy load for anyone, let alone a young lad like you.'

'Yeah,' he shrugged, still looking down.

'I can help, you know. Parklands is here for you and your mum. We've got some initiatives, you see, to help families when they hit a rough patch.'

I explained to him about our food bank and the emergency fund – resources we've put in place for times just like these kindly donated by businesses. His eyes widened slightly, still wary but tinged with a glimmer of hope.

'Here's the deal, Stewie. You focus on your school work and being the fantastic kid I know you are, and we'll help your family out. We're a team.'

I saw the clouds in his eyes part just a bit. 'Okay,' he nodded, very tentatively.

'Now, let's get you back to class, yeah?'

We walked back, and my heart felt ten pounds lighter, even if there was still work to be done. That chat was just the beginning. We got in touch with his mum, sorted out some immediate help and threw our collective arms around that family through our community programmes.

The next few days weren't a miraculous turnaround, let me tell you. Stewie had habits like barbs stuck in his coat. But the shifts, those ripples of change, started to surface soon enough.

Midweek, Miss Nolan, his class teacher, caught up with me during a break. 'Chris, you won't believe it! Stewie completed his entire writing task today – first time in ages... and he is the Times Tables Champion this week and he can't wait to represent 5N in the #BestSeatsInTheHouse assembly on Friday!'

She had this triumphant look, the kind that makes this job worth every sleepless night. And right there, you see, was the magic of respect blended with love. Not the flashy, shout-from-the-rooftops kinda love, but the steady, reliable, 'I'm here through thick and thin' type.

By the end of the month, we saw a different Stewie. More smiles, more focus, fewer outbursts. It wasn't just about cracking down on bad behaviour but understanding the stories and struggles behind them.

When you wade through the muck with these kids, honour their journeys, and provide a safe harbour, that's when real transformation happens. It's not textbook stuff, but it's raw, heart-stirring life.

Here's the essence – respect and love go hand in glove. We can plaster walls with rules, but it's those unspoken gestures, the respect given, the love extended, that really sculpt a child's world. That chilly Monday? It wasn't just about improving Stewie's behaviour, it was about revealing his capability for great things. All he needed was a little respect and a lot of heart.

Remember – sometimes, it just takes seeing the world through a child's eyes to help them see their own greatness.

Until next time, keep spreading the love!

I have visited a great many schools all over the UK, and I can honestly say that when I visited Parklands, on one of the most deprived estates in the UK, the love and care which the staff showed to pupils was an example to us all.

Anyway, back to dealing with mavericks…

Behaviour management is a 'team sport'

Again, this is apparent in both Paul and Tom's work and should be blindingly obvious.

And yet, many of us could point to that member of staff who likes to play fast and loose with the school's behaviour code. The maverick who 'is a mate' to the kids. Who likes to bend the rules. Who isn't a team player. Who may be very charismatic.

These people let their children talk loudly walking down the corridor because, hey it's just a rule – and rules are there to be broken! The children will love this maverick. Their colleagues won't.

Both Paul and Tom (and anyone who has spent any time teaching) will know that this maverick will sow the seeds of poor behaviour across the school. 'Why should I/we walk down the corridor when Mr/Mrs X's class don't have to?' goes up the cry.

Allow this maverick to strut about and the whole team culture is compromised.

Back to the 'fight phone'

By the time I reached the playground a large crowd had gathered to watch the (almost daily) spectacle. In the middle of the ring of bodies, two Year 5 boys were engaged in a proper full-on fight.

'Fight! Fight! Fight!' chanted the mob.

The Lunch Break Supervisors tutted from the side-lines but seemed to be unwilling to do anything to stop this clearly dangerous and inappropriate behaviour.

Janis (who had handed me the fight phone earlier), gestured frustratingly at the arena as she saw me.

'There it is Mr Botten – FIGHT!'

She, along with all the other adults were consumed by a powerlessness which had been learned over many similar scenarios, where their attempts to intervene had been futile and not supported by school leaders.

Separating the boys was relatively simple. They weren't even that cross with one another. This, like playing football, was just another playground activity which had become commonplace. However, getting them to follow me inside proved to be trickier…

One child, sensing that the new headteacher was planning to make a stand on this, headed straight to my office. The other laughed at my command and headed off with his mates to continue the game of football, all the while watched by a hundred children and a dozen staff, all watching what the new guy would do.

I gave him two minutes' take-up time. Nothing.

I used a passive body stance and a slow and low tone in talking calmly with him. He just carried on playing football.

I walked back to my office and when I emerged 20 minutes later he was surprised to see that I was carrying his coat and bag… and was accompanied by his mother.

Now, I don't believe that suspension is something which should be done lightly. It should be a last resort. But in a school where the culture had become so dangerous and so violent, it seemed like the only recourse to reset expectations.

In all I suspended 22 children in my first term as headteacher, most for a single day, all for similar violence and refusal to follow direct instructions. In my second term I suspended five children. In my third two. By my fourth term, I no longer needed to suspend at all.

I made fighting a red line. If you got into a fight your parents would be called. If you refused to stop, you'd be going home. I made sure all the parents and children knew this was a red line for me, so that there would be no surprises if someone chose to break this rule. I invested time in making sure that all staff showed unconditional positive regard with the mantra 'we care for you so much that we won't allow anyone to get hurt or to stop you learning'. A clear, simple behaviour code was adopted and regularly revisited. We started building a better, more attractive, school gang.

And I immediately 'misplaced' the fight phone. It was never used again.

Key takeaways

1. As headteacher, you decide the behavioural norms in your school – be brave!

2. Children want to feel part of a gang – make sure your school gang is the best gang.

3. Teach good behaviour – and call out good behaviour wherever you see it.

4. Like children unconditionally: reward and sanction proportionately and consistently.

5. *'Behaviour management is a team sport'* – Paul Dix.

Reflection tasks

Audit which children attend clubs and other activities and which don't. Cross-reference this with their level of attendance and their conduct. Is there a link between a lack of belonging and low attendance/ poor behaviour?

_____
_____
_____
_____
_____

Stop the first ten adults or children who you come across in school. Can they tell you the school rules?

_____
_____
_____
_____
_____

When and how do staff 'teach behaviour expectations'? Are staff given guidance on how and when to do this?

_____
_____
_____
_____
_____

How clearly does your behaviour policy promote positive behaviours? Is it explicit that these are being rewarded? Can children tell you what positive behaviour led to a particular reward?

_____
_____
_____
_____
_____

Is the school clear about its 'red lines'? Are these known by the pupils, parents and staff?

_____
_____
_____
_____
_____

Chapter 5

School improvement

A hundred tiny steps, without the BS

'Well Simon…. That wasn't good… not good at all!'

The LA's School Improvement Advisor closed her leather-bound notebook in a manner which I knew was imbided with both disappointment and irritation.

With the staff.

With the school.

And with me in particular.

I looked out at the February rain through my office window. I had been headteacher for about ten months and this was the second of the LA's 'Teaching & Learning Reviews' which saw a team of advisors descend on the school and decide whether we were still a 'cause for concern' (spoiler: we were).

'Teaching across the school is still too poor. Standards are too low.'

It was 2008 and these were the days when LAs had almost unparalleled power and influence. School Improvement Advisors were the Commissars and Inquisitors of these mighty organisations and held the fate of the headteachers and schools which they oversaw entirely in their hands. School improvement was developing as a discipline, supported by government cash, but often leaders were given very short timescales in which to get results (typically little over a year). And with a plentiful supply of wannabe headteachers, if one didn't work out, well, then the powers-that-be could simply get another.

'It's been nearly a year. Things need to improve faster.'

'We have done a lot. But it takes time,' I protested.

The LA Commissar looked out at the rain.

'You see Simon… You've now had two poor reviews…'

She put her notebook into her briefcase.

'One poor review is to be expected, given the "problems" with this place.'

She stood up and put on her coat.

'But two and... well...'

She paused.

'Two and we begin to wonder...'

And with that she left.

*

Improving a school is your main job as a school leader.

Whilst the peculiarities of accountabilities may have shifted slightly over the last twenty years, the fact remains that, as one experienced headteacher told me when I was applying for jobs, 'As Head, everything that happens in the school is your responsibility and your fault.'

I also think school improvement is one of the most exciting and interesting parts of the role and have been fortunate enough to have been able to improve schools, both in both substantive headships and in three executive head roles. And, whilst not exactly a science, school improvement is a field of study with ample research to draw upon.

But it does mean doing the right things in the right order.

There is a myriad of research articles, books and private consultants/snake oil salespeople, who will happily tell you, with great certainty, the best way to improve a school. And I would certainly suggest reading about this more deeply. However, from my experience, these are the most important bits to consider...

Understand your school before trying to improve it

I have seen many headteachers who, in a rush to crack on with school improvement, bang out a new three year strategic plan within a fortnight of being in post. The problem with this is that they're likely to have picked, at best, superficial and reactive goals (based usually on some duff data from a subject or statutory test), or at worst, applied their conformation bias to pick the things which they personally would like to improve or which they feel confident in improving (probably because they were previously in charge of improving them elsewhere).

Creating a new long term plan (usually three years) is impossible until you have spent time getting to know how the school and its teaching systems perform.

So spend the first few months getting into the weeds of self-evaluation. Call in others with fresh eyes to help you with this task. Work out which parts of the school's operation drive progress, and which need your attention. And do this in parallel with your re-visioning: thinking deeply about what the community wants, and needs, the school to be in the long term.

Create a short-term, (either a 100-day rapid improvement plan or a single year development plan) quickly by all means – as these seek to address clear immediate and short-term problems – but keep the long-term plan until you know and understand what the long term needs to look like.

Linking it to the vision

You should be able to draw a straight line from your vision statement to your school development plan.

If the school's vision is the 'why' and the mission is the 'how', these must be at the core of the school's long-term improvement plan.

If your vision and mission are articulated well, then all your school priorities, both short and long-term, should relate directly back to the school which the vision seeks to create. If you find it difficult to reference the vision in your school improvement strategy then, chances are, your vision is woolly or poorly articulated.

Separate short-term issues from long-term goals

There are short-term problems which take no more than a year to solve (often only a couple of months).

There are reactive goals, focusing on systemic existing problems, which take up to three years to achieve.

There are proactive goals, focusing on creating something new, which also take (at least) three years to achieve.

Then there is a whole heap of other 'stuff' which various people will tell you is a priority but actually isn't. In his excellent book *Lessons from the Head's Office*, Brian Walton describes this last category as 'Leadershit' (2023).

Having spent time truly understanding the school through deep self-evaluation, and having created a strong compelling vision and mission which acts both as shorthand for all the school is trying to improve and as a call-to-arms for all stakeholders, you need to sort all the priorities which you have come across into these three piles before you can start creating a coherent school improvement strategy.

It is likely you'll have several obvious short-term problems (dodgy Year 1 phonics outcomes, ropey writing in EYFS, etc.) which need to be addressed this year as they risk future learning (and Ofsted getting shirty with you). Unless these are rooted in a deeper systemic problem linked to teaching and learning across the school, a simple single-year implementation plan will sort these out. (More on this later.)

It is likely you'll have uncovered two or three big systemic issues which relate to educational standards. If you keep digging into these, you may find that the origin of these is actually one, over-arching problem. Either way, these are problems which will need several years of research, training and development to solve.

It is also likely that your vision and mission will demand that the school does things which it never did before. These priorities require you to strike out in new directions to make the school vision on paper become the school in actuality. These are the proactive goals – goals which you have chosen because they serve the vision directly.

Write a long list of all the priorities

(Apart from the 'leadershit' – ignore this).

Once you've assembled your priorities, you need to make some strategic decisions. There will be any number of things which you 'could' do to improve the school, but you have to whittle these down to a number which allows you to truly focus on them. As Jim Collins, author of *Good to Great* (2001), noted: 'If you have more than three priorities, you don't have any.'

So start by writing a list of the ten priorities which you have for the school for the next three years. Put to one side the short-term problems, as you can address maybe one of these a year on top of the long-term priorities.

Then it's time to make some decisions.

Which three (and only three) are you going to really commit to tackling in the next three years? It's likely here that you'll identify some which actually fit better under one over-arching priority statement. Complete this exercise with your SLT. Write the priorities on paper and argue their ordering out as a team. Priority 1 should be the most important thing that the school can commit to over all else, followed by Priorities 2 and 3. Everything else will have to wait.

Refine your three priorities into crafted goals

Once you have whittled your priorities down to just three, you now need to shape these from woolly ideas into carefully crafted goal statements. For this I tend to phrase my statements in two parts: the 'what' and the 'so what'. The 'what' says what you plan to do, the 'so what' articulates what the desired outcome on children will be.

Having recently completed this exercise at my two schools, at Blackhorse (with a long-standing vision and mission) we settled for the following:

- **Priority 1**: Further embed a culture of high expectations and challenge (the what) so that pupils demonstrate high levels of resilience and intrinsic motivation (the 'so what').

- **Priority 2**: Further develop the teaching of writing so that more pupils achieve or exceed the expected standard.

- **Priority 3**: Refine the remaining foundation subjects so that pupils can retain, recall and apply knowledge across all subjects.

Note that the wording is broad in places and more specific in others. As a school with a long-established and successful vision, with good outcomes, the word 'further' indicates that it is built on what went before. Schools with a newer vision, like my other school Emersons Green, may need to articulate a goal which is entirely new, so 'Create a culture of high expectations and challenge, so that pupils demonstrate resilience and intrinsic motivation' would be more appropriate.

Priority 1 links directly to the school's vision of 'Building Champion Learners through personal effort' and was a reactive goal to address a decline in resilience and intrinsic motivation (along with attendance) which we had seen in some of our children post-Covid. Priority 2 (also a reactive goal) aimed to address a systemic weakness in writing outcomes (when compared to reading and maths) and linked directly to the school's vision of 'building Champion Learners through expert tuition'. Priority 3 (a proactive goal) aimed to focus on building new way to help pupils retain core knowledge by both strengthening curriculum teaching and assessment opportunities, linking to the school's vision again in 'Building Champion Learners through both expert tuition and purposeful practice'.

Identify key actions and performance milestones

Having identified your three long-term goals, you next need to articulate what it means to have achieved this goal in as much precise detail as possible. For this, you will need to create a list of key actions (what you plan to do) and Key Performance Indicators (how you will know that you have succeeded) for the end of the first, second and third years of the strategic plan.

Here, it is easiest to start at the end of the final third year of the strategic plan and work backwards. Start by considering what total success 'looks' like. What will the children be achieving as a result of meeting this goal? What data would suggest you'd been successful? The Key Performance Indicators (KPIs) will look different for areas (such as maths) which have hard data behind them to others where less data exists, but you should try and be as precise as possible about what you think success will look like. Next, create KPIs for this first year of the plan. Finally, add in KPIs which sensibly bridge the first and final year for the second year of the plan.

When it comes to adding key actions to each year on the plan, it is likely that they will be more than a little vague in places – and this is to be expected (sometimes actually preferred). At this point when writing your plan, it would be unwise to second-guess the details of which strategies you will ultimately use to meet the goal. You may already researched some strategies and feel confident to include them on the plan, but please don't just 'grab for solutions' at this point. It is better to sit with a problem for longer, researching solutions so that you find the best one, than adopting something that another school has done and simply hoping for the best.

Creating annual plans for each priority

This is the point in the process which looks most similar to the traditional school development planning of old which most leaders are used to. However, having spent a couple of years using the EEF's implementation planning format (Education Endowment Foundation, 2024), I feel that it is far more useful than the old-fashioned 'action, resource, monitoring' format of old.

Step 1 of this approach involves really unpicking the problem, listing how the problem manifests itself for pupils (in terms of outcomes) and staff (in terms of practice). For example, in the 'improving writing' goal which we referenced earlier, statements like '*the % of pupils achieving GDS has declined post-Covid because of gaps in grammar and cohesion*' were noted under problems relating to pupil outcomes, whilst '*staff confidence in teaching composition and effect is varied across the school*' is noted in the problems for practice. In all, in this example, a total of five key problems are identified, which help us understand what we need to improve in more detail than simply noting that 'writing needs to improve'.

Step 2 then moves to the final two columns on the plan: implementation outcomes (how practice will have changed) and pupil outcomes (what difference this makes to pupils). These are split into three boxes for the end of terms two, four and six (end of year). Starting at the end of the year (and referencing back to the KPIs from the three year summary) add, with as much clarity as possible, what will have changed in terms of outcomes and practice at the end of the year. You then repeat this for the end of terms two and four, creating milestones which are, again, as unambiguous as possible.

Step 3 involves planning the actions. This is where the EEF's Guide to Implementation (2024) becomes essential reading (it's free online, so go read it!). It details far better than I the process of planning to implement a school improvement change. And whilst I won't repeat what it says here (go read it for yourself) a key takeaway is that *half* of the total implementation time should be taken up with the 'Explore stage' – examining the problem and researching possible solutions; and the 'Prepare stage' – planning, designing and preparing for the change (you do this by ensuring that those leading it really understand and are ready to train others effectively). It is therefore fine for up to half the school year to be spent on these two stages. If you've not worked this way before then it will feel worryingly slow but, as we'll come onto later, this will avoid poor, short-term and misunderstood decision-making.

The third stage in the EEF's implementation process is the delivery stage – the training which we are all used to. However, I have lost count of how many schools who

Problem (why?)	Change in practice (what?)	Implementation activities (how?) [including costs and resources]	Implementation outcomes (how well?) [milestones towards achieving goal]	Final/pupil outcomes (and so?) [intended goal for pupils]
Teaching There is not currently an overview of non-fiction teaching across the school. The modelling of writing is not yet embedded and there are inconsistencies in teachers' use of live modelling in writing lessons. Oracy and vocabulary are taught, but haven't been codified in a whole-school approach. Teachers do not have secure knowledge of genre progression within non-fiction writing. Adaptive teaching strategies are not always used to support children not yet able to access year-group curriculum. Learning [...]	2A Active ingredient: *Design and implement a clear teaching sequence for writing in EYFS, Y1 and Y6:* - Evaluate and update current English teaching through evidence-based research - Provide opportunities for children in EYFS and Y1 to embed transcriptional skills - Teach using opportunities for oracy, modelled writing and dictated sentences in EYFS and Y1 - Teach using opportunities for revising to up-level writing in Y6 2B Active ingredient: *Adapt and embed non-fiction progression document:* - Align non-fiction progression with partnership goals and grammar teaching - Ensure coverage of all non-fiction genres within each year group 2C Active ingredient: [...]	Develop materials: - BH — Non-fiction coverage document across each year group - Partnership non-fiction progression document - Codified teaching sequence for EYFS, Y1 and Y6 - Example of Excellence for each non-fiction text type for each year group Deliver training: - Non-fiction progression document - Live modelling of non-fiction writing (staff meetings, model lessons) - Adaptive teaching strategies for children not working at age-related expectation - EYFS/Y1 teachers: teaching sequence and the use of dictated sequences - Leaf training: teaching writing - Leaf training: developing greater depth writing - Leaf training: developing language into developing early writing (EYFS) Coaching - Instructional coaching in live modelling for all teachers - Instructional coaching for adaptive teaching strategies (teachers and teaching assistants)	End of term 2 Fidelity: - All teachers are using live modelling throughout the teaching sequence - EYFS and Y1 teachers are beginning to use a codified approach to the teaching of transcription skills Acceptability: - EYFS and Y1 teachers understand the importance of transcriptional skills ahead of compositional skills - Staff understand the importance of live modelling Reach: - Pupils in EYFS and Y1 are being taught through a codified approach to transcription - All children are experiencing live modelling in their writing lessons End of term 4 [...]	Short term: end of term 2 Pupils can talk about the format of different genres of non-fiction writing. Pupils in EYFS and Y1 are being taught through a codified approach to transcription and are having opportunities to practise these key skills. Pupils are experiencing quality-first teaching of writing through live modelling and working walls. Medium term: end of term 4 [...]

claim to have implemented a new strategy and are dumbfounded when it didn't stick, only to admit, when pressed, that they maybe only devoted an INSET and possibly a single follow-up staff meeting to it. Change takes time and numerous staff meetings!

Finally, the EEF's final stage, which will probably fill the final two terms, is the 'Sustain' stage. This focuses on embedding and refining (again, more on this later).

Turning your plan into action

For me, my 'Raising Attainment Plan' (RAP) is perhaps the single most useful tool for school improvement planning, but it is often forgotten by headteachers newer to the role as I don't think it's currently taught in headteacher school (NPQH or suchlike).

Originally part of the DfE's Improving Schools Programme (2008), a government scheme in the late noughties aimed at improving struggling and underperforming schools (like mine was in 2007), it included training and tools to help heads improve schools in the short and long term. One of these was the RAP.

Much like a Blue Peter craft project, to make your RAP you will need a pile of different coloured sticky notes, a large display board, some sharpies and a ruler. The RAP consists of a grid with each square big enough for a sticky note. Along the top (x axis) of the grid we have the weeks of the term – one column for each week; down the side (y axis) we have swim-lanes for the different priorities, starting with Priority 1 as it's the most important. After the three priorities, I also have swim-lanes for:

- 'maintenance monitoring' (all the stuff which you need to be sure is happening right)
- one for the data and pupil progress meetings
- one for staff meetings,
- one for business actions and
- one for SLT meetings.

The column on the far right is left for milestones – the KPIs which you carefully crafted earlier – although you'll only need these for your three priorities.

Then you go back to your implementation plan and allocate all the research, training, coaching, monitoring and so to a week (we'll come to this later), focusing on what needs to be completed to meet your KPIs at the end of the first two terms. This breaks down the big, scary goals into tiny little manageable steps.

'But wouldn't this be better as a spreadsheet?' I hear you cry. (And the answer is 'yes' – I also have mine on a spreadsheet). However, the idea of having it on sticky notes, ideally in a room where your SLT meet, is that it keeps the RAP the 'main thing'. The focus of all SLT meetings should be on driving school improvement – not getting bogged down in 'leadershit' as can so quickly happen. Having the RAP on the wall makes sure it is the first thing leaders see each day. Sticky notes can also be moved – and invariably your best-laid plans will need to change so being able to pick them up and move them helps. The different coloured sticky notes help, especially when it comes to planning in the staff meetings. Because you have them in the same corresponding colour as the priority (1, 2 or 3), you can see at a glance whether you are actually devoting most of your most precious training time to the most pressing priorities.

As a new MAT, the Leaf Trust tried to focus leaders on this discipline of school improvement. I have worked with Ross, previously a successful headteacher and now the Trust's CEO, for over a decade, and his clarity on school improvement is exceptional. Here's his take on the process…

Case Study: Ross Newman

CEO of the Leaf Trust

In my career, I have been privileged and lucky enough to lead schools as headteacher and executive headteacher and support other schools' improvement journey as an advisor. Now, I am beyond privileged to lead a family of schools as CEO of a trust. Throughout this time in school leadership, I have come to hold the following as true:

- **School improvement is hard!** It requires considerable effort and resources, day after day, week after week, term after term, year after year.
- **School improvement is a field of practice of its own**. It is a set of observable and teachable skills and behaviours separate from broader leadership and management.
- School improvement is what Simon Sinek would describe as an **'infinite game'**. There is no endpoint, and the players often change, as do the rules. It is a continuous cycle.
- **True, embedded, lasting change takes time**.
- **School improvement is a team game**. Its success or failure, its ability to last beyond a change in personnel relies on a team approach.
- It works best with a **clearly articulated and understood model**.

Early in my first headship, I introduced a new initiative, led staff training sessions and made some shiny documentation to support the initiative, and it was a complete failure! It failed because I went straight into implementation and did not pay enough attention to building the foundations; therefore, I built on foundations of sand. I had broken Jim Collins's number one rule

---

and had focused first on 'what' rather than 'who'. Now I know that for success and to make deep, lasting change, I always, and I do mean always, start first with 'who' and then 'what'.

As social media has grown in influence and popularity over the past ten years, we are becoming increasingly exposed to images of perfection and the finished product. It is easy to see only the finished beautiful product and to try to skip the hard groundwork and jump to the more glossy 'quick fixes'. It can often appear to the outside world that a school's success is a revolutionary and sudden breakthrough. This is contrary to reality from the inside.

With my commitment to our trust, I started looking for a model I could develop and use to help schools move forward as a team. The model needed to support a people-first approach and help them visualise and understand that school improvement is hard work and incremental and that no one thing alone suddenly and miraculously improves a school. I found the model I was looking for, not in the world of education but in business: The Flywheel. In his book *Good to Great*, Jim Collins details the use of a flywheel approach (2001). Like the one found in a car or potter's wheel, a flywheel takes a lot of energy to get going, but this heavy disc builds momentum and drives forward once in motion. It evens out the energy applied, meaning the wheel keeps turning without losing power, if you must focus on one area for a while. Collins details how a flywheel approach can be developed by doing the 'right things' in the 'right order', again and again, turn by turn, building momentum, and strategically building on successes. He asserts that by doing the first thing on the flywheel, you are compelled to do the next and the next.

I spent a long time thinking about what I believed would be the right things and even more time thinking about the right order. So here is what I came up with:

1. Appoint dedicated staff committed to continuous growth: the right people in the right roles,
2. Build collaborative improvement teams and culture,
3. Align your team towards shared vision and values,
4. Design an ambitious, joyful curriculum for all to succeed (what),
5. Establish compelling frameworks (how),
6. Establish predictable routines and expectations and build relationships,
7. Invest in advancing and developing staff knowledge and skills,
8. Consistently implement the curriculum, pedagogies and compelling frameworks,

9. Develop the use of timely assessment to drive future learning,
10. Embed a culture of excellence for all, evaluating and refining practice,
11. Use outcomes to drive priorities for improvement and celebration,
12. Develop passionate new leaders and replenish the workforce pipeline.

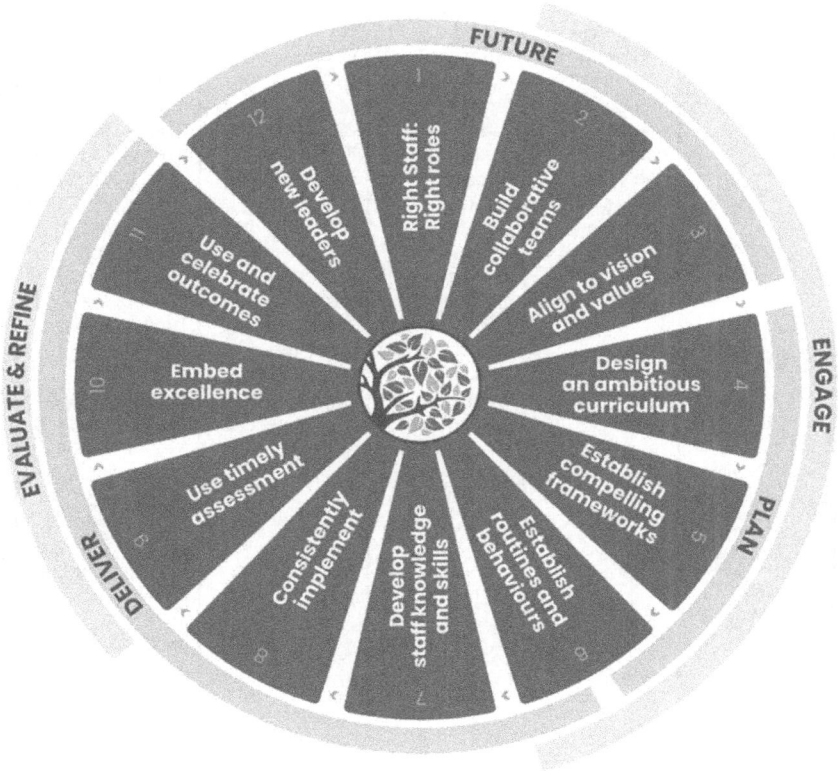

FIGURE 1 The Leaf Trust Flywheel

Inspired by the flywheel model, I was led to *Unleash Your Transformation: Using the Power of the Flywheel to Transform Your Business* by Marco Van Kalleveen and Peter Koijen (2022). In this book, the authors explore applying four levels of power to each of the flywheel elements. Once a shared understanding and commitment to this approach was established, I could write descriptors of power at each level with my team. An example is given below.

Level of Power	No Power	Some Power	Good Power	Transformational Power
3. Align your team towards shared vision and values	**Unknown Purpose:** No or outdated statements exist. But these are not known by staff or pupils. They are not referenced and do not guide decision-making. Staff are pulling in different directions.	**Purpose on Paper:** A purpose statement, vision and values are written down and highlighted around the school and on the school website. Some pupils and staff know it, but is not a source of motivation or inspiration. It does not guide decision-making or behaviours.	**Living Purpose:** A clear and compelling purpose, vision and set of values are developed by a wide group within the school. It is widely communicated, and staff, parents and pupils can recall it when asked. It is referenced when planning but does not always guide decisions.	**Passionate Purpose:** All develop the school's shared vision, and it acts as a golden thread throughout all aspects of school life. Its impact is tangible. Vision and values in church schools are rooted in theological understanding and enabling in their application. The school's purpose, vision and values guide long-term decision-making, even when it is challenging. The values are felt by all. The school's vision, values and mission promote courageous advocacy. Justice and responsibility as ethical agents of change are key drivers within the school vision.

We now use this model as the foundation for all our school improvement work. By doing the 'right things' in the 'right order' and improving on each turn of our flywheel, we build momentum, compounding our successes, eventually hitting a point where we move from build-up to break-through.

The model's success is not necessarily the model itself but the in power of having a shared and understood language for school improvement. It supports our culture of people first and helps visualise that school improvement is hard, a team game, and that no one thing in isolation will achieve the transformation we are after. To accomplish a flywheel, the levels of power need to be equal on each element; this has helped schools develop an incremental approach and ensure secure improvement before going back to the start to develop the next level of power. The approach also enabled us to design professional development focusing on each of the twelve elements for new and aspiring leaders.

I am not claiming that this model will work for everyone or that it is perfect, but it has worked well in the schools I have led and now in the trust I lead. My key message is whichever approach you take, learn it, embrace it, and stick to it without deviation. You will never know if it is a strategy or leadership which succeeds or fails if you take an inconsistent approach, but the flywheel works for us.

Within our Trust, this model is used for all school improvement conversations and is keeping us all focused on consistently doing what we know works.

Finally, chew the elephant

Before finally irrevocably ruining one of my joints on the Green Man Ultramarathon course in 2021, my favoured hobby involved completing running races which varied between 30 and 60 miles in length, usually over wild parts of the country. The scale of the distances were frightening and would, at times, seem impossible. However, ultrarunners learn to 'chew the elephant'. 'How do you eat an elephant?' the saying goes. 'One bite at a time'.

And that, dear reader, is where 99% of school improvement work falls down. School leaders often assume that practice can change overnight, as the result of an inspirational speaker at an INSET or a single staff meeting. In reality, it takes a long time to truly change and embed practice. You have to take that big goal and break it into hundreds of tiny components. You have to sequence these components into a logical order: 'Explore, Prepare, Deliver, Sustain'. Then you have to enact these elements one after the other, after the other, for weeks, and months and terms and (for really big goals) years. The things which are truly strong and consistent in my schools took over a decade for us to develop.

The key is to be consistent and persistent in your enactment of school improvement plans.

And what of the grumpy LA Commissar?

I would love to tell you that a term after the grumpy LA Commissar suggested my job was on the line I had, through a combination of ferocious talent and dashing good looks, aced an Ofsted inspection and transformed the school.

But that would be a myth.

It is true to say that within two years the school had achieved its first 'Good' judgement in a decade and results which put it at the top of the league tables.

But this was achieved by a lot of kind advice from others and the ever watchful eye of the LA Commissar, who, incidentally, went on to build a crop of headteachers who now run some of the most successful schools in the city.

It would also be wrong to conclude the school improvement story there, with this dashingly young and ferociously talented headteacher having saved the day. However, I would leave the school for a 'bigger' headship within six months of the successful Ofsted. The school would stay at the top of the league tables for a further two years… and then dropped right back to near the bottom. Within five years of me leaving it would once again be judged 'Requires Improvement'. Like the now thoroughly debunked 'super-head' model of improvement, which sees a charismatic leader sweep in and rapidly improve outcomes before riding off into the sunset, my ambitions would prove to be a mile wide and an inch deep.

As I said, it takes a long time to truly improve a school. Something I would spend the next ten years trying to achieve.

Key takeaways

1. You should be able to draw a straight line from your school vision to your School Development Plan. If you can't, one (or both) is wrong.

2. Separate priorities from 'Leadershit'.

3. Remember that 'If you have more than three priorities then you don't have any priorities' (Jim Collins, 2001).

4. Operationalise your goals by turning them into weekly actions and termly milestones.

5. Genuine school improvement takes time.

Reflection tasks

Take a highlighter pen and highlight every part of your current long- and short-term school improvement plans which link back to your school's vision. Does your plan drive your vision forward?

List all your current priorities, alongside your evidence that they are actually a priority. Rank them in order. Sort them into three piles: Reactive Goals, Proactive Goals and Short-term Problems. Does your current School Improvement Plan adequately address these?

_____

_____

_____

_____

_____

If your school's priorities are already clearly defined, look at the Key Performance Indicators which you have set to define their success, both in the short and long term. Are these clear and measurable?

_____

_____

_____

_____

_____

Again, if your school's priorities are already known and shared, stop the first ten staff members that you come across tomorrow and ask them what they are.

If you already have a RAP, look carefully: are the main priorities given most of the staff training time? Have you built in sufficient time to explore and prepare for new initiatives?

_____

_____

_____

_____

_____

Chapter 6
Improving teaching
Making the invisible visible

'It's *actual* brain science!' I announced proudly and with a fervent tone that only a zealous new deputy headteacher in their twenties could muster at the first INSET they were allowed to lead.

It was 2003 and 'Accelerated Learning' was all the rage amongst hip movers and shakers (like me) in at the forefront of this educational enlightenment.

I left a dramatic pause to let it sink in.

Nothing.

The hall full of (long-serving and experienced) staff seemed to care little for the revolution in 'science-led' learning techniques which I had spent the last hour regaling them with. The maths results were dodgy... so were the English results. Some staff had actually suggested that the INSET day should be used to learn how to teach maths better (oh, the poor simple souls). Which is why it was imperative that the most scientifically rigorous techniques known in the history of teaching should be rolled out without any further delay. How were children supposed to excel in maths if they weren't allowed to develop their understanding of fractions through playing volleyball? Had they never heard of 'kinaesthetic learners'?

I suspected they just weren't engaging their 'right brain' – the home, as we all know, of creative thought.

Luckily, I knew the neurological magic which would engage this side of the brain and get this INSET back on track... I was practically a brain surgeon!

'OK everyone,' I chimed, 'on your feet!'

'It's time to introduce you to Brain Gym!'

I would spend the next two years embedding accelerated learning techniques into every class in the school.

Sadly, we later discovered that the whole idea was complete bollocks.

*

How to improve teaching

I have been trying to change teaching and learning for the better since getting my first subject leader role (PE) in 1996.

As a headteacher, it has been the thing which has occupied more of my time and energy than anything else (and so it should, the clue is in the title).

Sometimes I have been successful and outcomes have improved.

Sometimes I have been unsuccessful and outcomes have stayed about the same (more on this later).

And sometimes I have been successful and outcomes have actually got worse (again, more on this later).

However, I do believe that teaching has improved dramatically since I started my career in the late nineties, when you could pretty much teach anything you wanted, however you pleased. I also believe that we live in a golden age of research into the science of teaching and learning, and that this research has never been more easily accessible to educators.

So, if improving outcomes for pupils, by improving teaching, is our number 1 priority, how do we do it?

Attend to the 'why'

First attend to the 'why' and establish psychological safety within the team.

For staff to buy in to school improvement, they need to know two things:

1. Why it is important to both the future of the school as a whole, and to them as individuals.

2. How safe they will be (professionally speaking) during the messy early phases of implementation when they are getting the new approach or technique more wrong than right.

As we discussed in the previous chapter, our school improvement priorities need to link back directly to the school's vision, which will have been developed in collaboration with the staff team. When this is the case, explaining the 'why' of any new initiative should be straightforward: it furthers the agreed vision of the school. Staff need to know the 'why' if they are to add to their (already exhaustive) workload and take on a new way of working. Yet all too often, leaders jump straight into explaining the 'what' and the 'how'.

It is also essential that staff feel professionally safe, in general, and specifically when new initiatives are being phased in. Sometimes, endeavours to improve teaching fail before they have even begun as a result of a deficit of trust amongst the team. In short, the team either have too little respect for the leader in order to follow them along a new path (which in my experience is quite rare), or they simply don't yet trust the leader enough to allow themselves to be vulnerable in front of them (which in my experience is more common).

We will discuss trust and the team in more depth later, but when considering any initiative, school leaders need to do the groundwork to build the necessary trust which will allow staff fully engage with the proposed change. In practical terms, this could be something as simple as being clear with staff that we are all learning together and that there will be no negative impact on the individual personally if they fail to master this new initiative straight away.

Again, this is no great insight; we all know that staff are more likely to successfully adopt a new approach when they feel safe and relaxed about their new learning: 'high challenge, low threat'. However, I also know that when schools are under pressure to improve quickly (as mine have been at times; the 'vibes' which leaders can give off can either overtly or covertly convey to the team that they are engaged in a 'high challenge, high threat' endeavour. And this never helps staff learn.

As Brené Brown (2018) so eloquently puts it: 'Leaders must either invest a reasonable amount of time attending to fears and feelings, or squander an unreasonable amount of time trying to manage ineffective and unproductive behaviour.'

Separate professional development from formal appraisal processes

For many years lesson observations, along with data, were used to assess whether teachers would pass their annual appraisal. These observations came with long forms and usually blunt judgement boxes to tick at the bottom, ranging from 'inadequate' to 'outstanding'. Teachers could (and sometimes were) placed on capability procedures if they taught a duff lesson. This high-stakes environment destroyed trust between school leaders and staff and resulted in teachers hiding any weaknesses for fear that it would come back to bite them when it came to their appraisal.

In my schools, as in all schools, staff are expected to meet the National Teaching Standards. However, we assume that they are, unless compelling evidence arises to suggest they aren't. It has been nearly a decade since any teacher was placed on formal capability procedures and given a (again, high-stakes) support plan.

But it has taken many years for me to gain the trust of staff whose unions are, understandably, very twitchy about lesson observations being used against their members. The thought of me walking into their classes weekly (as I now do) and sitting down to watch some teaching would have led to a riot a decade ago. Only by repeatedly telling staff that we are all trying to improve and that they won't be punished for not mastering something straight away, and then proving this to them by my actions over many years, have staff learned to trust leaders when we visit their classrooms.

It is essential leaders separate accountability measures from staff development.

Give leaders time to research the problem and all possible solutions

As we discussed in the last chapter, the key to improving teaching starts with a thorough analysis of the problem which you are trying to solve. If you are starting to tackle the problem at the start of an academic year, it may be that it takes the first two terms to really unpick exactly which parts of your teaching approach isn't working.

Again, this should sound like advice which wouldn't even warrant a mention, but time and time again schools, often driven by the need to quickly improve standards, grab for a solution without fully understanding the problem. This either leads to the school solving a problem which doesn't exist, or replacing a 'so-so' approach with a new, but less effective technique, resulting in standards actually declining.

One of the most impactful actions which I recently took to improve teaching and learning was to give the leader in charge of 'solving the problem' a day a week out of class to evaluate what exactly the problem was and then research possible solutions. I remember at the time thinking this was painfully slow: our brains are wired to prefer action (even the wrong action) to uncertainty. Seeing the English Leader sat for three months analysing evidence and data, visiting classes and talking to staff, and then researching and reading, seemed reckless (and expensive). However, it led to the most effective improvement, both in terms of the quality of training and the efficacy of the solution, that the school had ever seen.

But, again, it has taken me fifteen years of rushing headlong into premature action to understand that this rarely, if ever, creates the best results.

Avoid quick and easy solutions

I have been in the game long enough to smell bullshit.

And we as a profession, love a bit of glamorous crap. As Doug Lemov (2010) noted, *'One of the problems with teaching is that there's a temptation to evaluate what we do in the classroom based on how clever it is, how it aligns with a larger philosophy, or even how gratifying it is to use, not necessarily how effective it is in driving student achievement'*.

In our current educational biome, there are countless bloggers, authors (?!), consultants and social media 'edu-influencers' who speak with great certainty about the efficacy of their approach/product. Whilst I have no idea how effective the

'Cog-Sci' mob's ideas will be in twenty years' time, I see the same level of missionary zeal and absolute certainty as I did at the turn of the century when the (now largely de-bunked) Accelerated Learning fad swept through classrooms.

There will be genuinely good ideas put forward by genuinely reflective researchers.

There will be genuinely good ideas put forward by utter grifters out to make a fast buck.

And then there will be terrible ideas which are sold as the silver bullet to all your problems.

Sadly, whilst there is better educational research available to inform decision making than ever before, there is no such thing as 'best practice', only 'best bets'. Leaders need to carefully look at the available evidence to decide whether the proposed change will have the desired impact in their setting. Remember the Dylan Wiliam quote: *'Everything works somewhere; nothing works everywhere'*.

Before committing valuable time and resources into implementing an approach school-wide, check that it will actually work to solve your problem.

Create 'Research and Development' pilot teams

Whilst some improvements to teaching require a single leader to focus on finding a single 'best bet' for the school, where the solution (or even the nature of the problem) is less clear, and where timescales allow (e.g. this isn't an urgent problem which must be solved at pace), then harnessing the wider staff team to research and pilot different approaches can be hugely beneficial.

For the last few years, staff have had a common 'professional growth project' (linked to appraisal) where they are tasked with finding potential solutions to a problem which the school is struggling to solve. We have sought to answer questions such as 'how do we use spaced retrieval to help children remember more?'. It isn't a free for all – where staff can indulge a passion for teaching calculus exclusively through the medium of mime – the focus is set by the school leaders, seeking to solve a whole-school problem. Staff work in teams of three to five and select a particular approach to research and trial throughout the year. They are given research time during staff meetings and often a free book to kick-start their thinking. Indeed, if they want to spend the whole staff meeting reading during the first couple of terms then that is fine with me. They then complete 'lesson study' visits and appraise the impact of the technique on learners within the pilot classrooms. Finally, they present their findings back to their colleagues at the end of the year, allowing leaders to then take these findings, determine which were the 'best bets', and then work up a whole school policy or approach for the following year.

Whilst this is a slow way to improve teaching, it has a number of clear benefits. First, it allows the school to test possible solutions to problems prior to adopting an approach across the school. Second, it allows those irritating 'wrinkles' in the approach (which annoy teachers as they don't quite work in practice) to be ironed out through tweaking the approach during the pilot phase. Finally, and perhaps most importantly, it changes the school improvement culture within the team from 'done to' to 'done together', with staff gaining deep knowledge of an area of practice through their own action research, resulting in greater buy-in when the final 'best bet' is adopted.

Plan staff training carefully

Keep the main thing, the main thing.

Once a 'best bet' has been selected, it is essential that due consideration is given to how you as leaders will support staff in mastering this new approach to teaching. Whilst there has been much thought given to how we help students master new content (through careful sequencing and spaced practice within the curriculum), we often seem to completely ignore these principles when it comes to teaching staff to master new content or approaches themselves.

The traditional model for this has been a whole day INSET where staff are shown all the components of the new approach and are then simply instructed to 'make it so'. However, we know that this often leads to failure as there is simply too much content for staff to absorb in one go. Whilst it is sensible to prime staff for a big change to teaching with a whole day showing them the big picture, and even each constituent part, there then needs to be an implementation plan which breaks down the new teaching approach into its constituent parts which can then be taught to the staff one at a time.

Paul Bambrick-Santoyo, managing director of the Uncommon Schools Network, describes this process as '*See it, name it, do it*' (2012).

A successful implementation plan will train staff on each of the parts of the new approach through a combination of direct instruction (INSET delivered at staff meetings etc. – the 'see it' element) followed by codification (clear step-by-step written guidance on how to teach the new approach – the 'name it' element), followed by instructional coaching (the 'do it' element). This new knowledge is not all given in one go, but instead is sequenced and delivered to staff sequentially after enough time has passed to ensure that the previous step has been mastered.

This is where good initial school improvement planning on paper, via the Implementation Plan discussed in the previous chapter comes into play. If the new learning has been sequenced clearly on this plan, then it is relatively simple to then allocate available training time to the approach on the RAP (which we also discussed earlier). And remember – attaining mastery of a new technique is a process, not a singular event.

What we must not allow ourselves to do is cram our RAP with multiple new approaches and expect teachers to master them simultaneously. Typically staff can only master one new approach at a time, and this may take three or four months. If we try to introduce 'everything, all at once' (no matter how urgent the other stuff may be) we will confuse staff, wear them ragged and ultimately slow the process of improving teaching.

Don't be coy about codification

As leaders, we sometimes get a little coy about directing staff to teach in a particular way, afraid that it will stifle their professional creativity or autonomy. However, I have come to believe that staff feel happier when they are given clear frameworks to work within.

Historically, individual staff will have been observed teaching and then given vague advice such as 'improve questioning', which tells the teacher nothing about how they can do this, and certainly not what routine to use for eliciting good answers to questions. To improve teaching, we must break any teaching approach down into teachable, observable routines. We must codify practice and use consistent language to describe each tiny aspect of a teaching approach so that we can describe small details accurately.

Consider the teaching of Systematic Synthetic Phonics – arguably one of the most impactful changes to teaching of reading in the last ten years. It relies on complete fidelity to the scheme. There is no room for teacher creativity or autonomy. Every part of the session is given a specific name, the details of each part is articulated. Hand gestures for blending and segmenting etc. are the same in every classroom so the children instantly recognise this element as they move between classes.

The result? Consistency of practice and consistency of outcomes. It doesn't matter whether you've been teaching two years or twenty, the quality of phonics teaching is the same.

And whilst phonics has particularly rigid subject content which makes it ideal for such an approach, believe that similar codification of practice does have a place in other areas of teaching.

With our school partnership, we have adopted what we call our 'principles of expert tuition': five elements of teaching which we believe should be part of every lesson:

1. **What are we doing?** Defining the context of the lesson.
2. **Let's remember:** Recapping prior knowledge.

3. **Read it ourselves:** All new knowledge is first read by the children themselves.

4. **'I do, we do, you do':** Structured direct instruction and practice.

5. **Learning check:** Recapping today's key learning.

We have now gone one step further and provided staff with a 'slide deck template' which can be used for all lessons which structures all lessons using these five areas. Staff are expected to use these in humanities and science teaching, but increasingly have opted to use them in all other foundation subjects (maths and English have more subject-specific slide decks already). The result has been significant improvements in the quality (and consistency) of teaching of the foundation curriculum. Interestingly, subjects like PE and Art have benefitted the most from a simple, single structure giving shape to teachings. More interestingly still, teachers report that they enjoy teaching more and find planning easier as they aren't juggling different expectations and approaches for different subjects.

What's more, when it came to training staff on each of the five components, most of which came from previous staff-led research projects, each step was already clearly codified and defined, allowing staff and leaders to pinpoint areas for development more clearly. It made the 'invisible, visible'.

Again, this needs to be done with a great deal of thought. Some of us are old enough to remember the National Literacy Strategy of the late nineties where lesson structures were dictated centrally by the government, which was suffocating. However, if we have thoroughly trialled our 'best bets' and then trained staff well, codification is a logical step.

But before we go on, let's hear from another exceptional school leader, Claire Savory, who confronted her team's fears head on when called upon to improve teaching.

Case Study: Claire Savory

Ex-executive headteacher, National Leader of Education and CEO of the Gloucestershire Learning Alliance

Transformational school improvement is indeed a messy business. My leadership learning and initiation began when I was deployed by the local authority as the headteacher at an outstanding school to provide leadership as part of a team with two other successful heads, to turn around a school that had been judged as inadequate. This was a model that replicated the principles of a strong MAT and was an early example of an alternative leadership model that was seen to be innovative at the time.

Having checked the school website prior to starting, I marvelled at the irony of their messaging about being an 'EPIC' school. We found butterflies stuck to walls allegedly as positive symbols for school improvement. I later discovered that this idea had been taken from the London Challenge initiative which orchestrated structural 'system-led' school to school improvement. It is based on the principle that a single, seemingly insignificant act, such as a butterfly wing flapping its wings, can serve as a catalyst, impacting large scale change from seemingly insignificant beginnings. These felt laughably out of place.

The general view from staff was that Ofsted had got it wrong – 'they (the inspectors) were a tough team and just didn't get us'. Cue the change curve… The local authority called a meeting with all staff to challenge this perception in the most direct way. It was the most uncomfortable meeting where tough messages were delivered. My only slight distraction was noticing the green hue from my colleague headteacher who had been less than successful in removing the effects of being in role as Shrek for World Book Day.

The change curve has become an invaluable tool in my leadership toolkit ever since. I use it in any change scenario to support how staff can visualise and articulate their emotional responses to the change, whether this is introducing a new validated phonics scheme, responding to the appointment of a new head teacher, or an Ofsted disappointment. It can help staff to see how they risk being stuck in shock and denial and see how this will limit the forward momentum of the necessary improvement journey.

Speaking of shock, my first day on site in the failing school was a complete shock, facing the reality of what an absence of high-quality leadership had done to a school, rendering it completely inadequate. The school didn't feel safe. Parents were angry. Naughty children were dealt with by the headteacher, and they were regularly sent to the office to be reprimanded (although this appeared to mean that they had a timeout with some toys?). The curriculum was a shambles, Early Years was depressing (I have never seen so many teddy bears) and teacher talk dominated every lesson. There was a paucity of appropriate resources and teachers were using flipcharts in front of their interactive whiteboards because they didn't know how to use them.

I learnt very quickly that whilst culture absolutely does eat strategy for breakfast, we also needed a suite of clear policies, systems and practices to keep everyone safe and to enable effective accountability. Staff development became a key focus and we adopted an immersive approach. We introduced mandatory weekly staff training sessions (with optional extras) to model the approaches we were looking for, making meaning of the newly introduced teacher standards.

As almost all the teaching was inadequate, we had to bring the role-modelling cavalry from the three supporting schools. We buddied all the teachers up with peer-teacher-mentors from the three supporting schools to help to develop their planning, quality resources, and the delivery. Critically, this included time in each other's classrooms as well as remote support for planning. Plans were sent to mentors who reviewed them and provided feedback including sharing their own ideas and resources where possible. This peer-to-peer approach had reciprocal benefits for all the teachers involved, learning from each other in the business of crafting lessons. To put it simply, we were fostering a culture where thinking and talking about curriculum and pedagogy was encouraged. Children first, not staff first. Now that's *epic*!

Developing and retaining great teachers was an incredible challenge. We had to be so committed and relentless in our mission and it often felt as though we were taking multiple steps backwards, particularly as the staff absence and turn-over accelerated in the first waves of school improvement.

I learnt more about myself as a leader in the business of transformation and school improvement than I did in achieving the coveted Ofsted 'outstanding'. This gritty, gnarly, messy work enabled me to discover my leadership potential. Learning from other experienced colleagues, building capacity through collaborative practice and really noticing what makes the biggest difference for children.

'Your leadership past does not define your future, and therein lies the possibility.'

France Frei and Anne Morriss, *Unleashed* (2020).

Claire clearly demonstrates how culture and pedagogy go hand in hand.

And now back to something more mundane – teachers' medium-term planning!

Knowledge and experience

Ensure those completing long-term plans have the experience and knowledge to do so.

Like many schools, we have spent a great deal of time over the last five years reorganising our curriculum. And, like many schools, we have (on many occasions) found that sequences of lessons (especially in foundation subjects) have lacked the cohesion and precision which we hoped for.

After spending many years grappling with this problem, we concluded that it was very difficult for a new teacher, or one new to a particular year, to perfectly pitch a sequence of lessons, with appropriately challenging learning tasks. Time and time again, our intent didn't match our implementation.

So now, medium term lesson plans in most of the foundation subjects are completed by the subject leader for all year groups. Where the subject leader is new themselves, a member of the SLT will work with them to create these 'skeleton plans'. It has had a dramatic impact on the quality of teaching and learning in these subjects. A single author can ensure cohesion and progression between units of work, with themes which may be revisited several years apart, seeing the 'grand sweep' of learning across the school as a whole. Teachers have to create their own individual lesson plans, but the heavy lifting has been done by someone else.

'But what of teacher autonomy and creativity?' you once again cry. However, our experience has been that teachers feel happier as they have one less task to complete, and can instead put their energies into ensuring the lessons are taught well – not trying to grab random resources on 'the heart' or 'mountains' off the internet, late on a Sunday evening.

If you want to improve teaching, especially in foundation subjects, make sure the person doing the planning is qualified to do so.

Embed new teaching approaches through Instructional Coaching

Instructional Coaching (Farndon, 2019) is perhaps the single most powerful tool for improving the quality of a teacher's practice (the 'do it' element). It is important to note that instructional coaching is not the same as traditional leadership coaching, where the coach asks a series of open questions but offers no solutions. Sadly, I have visited many schools which have adopted coaching (usually because it's a trendy thing to do) and are trying to support inexperienced teachers using a coaching model without telling them what they need to do to improve.

In the Instructional Coaching model, the coach is often the 'master' and the coachee the 'apprentice'. The Instructional Coach will usually already know how to use the new teaching approach successfully and will understand each of the codified steps well.

Once staff have been given direct training on the new teaching approach, Instructional Coaching usually begins a couple of weeks later, once the teachers has started trying to implement the approach within their classroom. The coach will observe the teacher using the new teaching approach for no more than five to ten minutes and will leave the moment that they see an aspect of the approach which could be more effectively delivered. They will then meet with the member of staff (again just for five minutes) and provide a highly specific target linked to the clearly codified teaching process which the teacher is trying to master. So instead of setting a generic target such as 'get the children to read more in your lessons' the coach will set a target such as 'In the 'read it ourselves' element of the lesson, make sure all the children follow the text with their fingers'. Such a specific target makes it virtually impossible for the teacher to fail to meet it when they are next observed by their coach the following week, which itself builds teacher confidence and furthers the 'high challenge, low threat' approach to school improvement. Moreover, often nothing is written down, or if it is, it is scribbled on a sticky: completely disposable and the complete opposite of high stakes formal written lesson observations of old. Sometimes, the coach will invite the coachee to observe that specific step within their own classroom and sometimes, the coach and coachee will practice a step in an empty classroom, without a 'live audience' of pupils. The coaching sessions will typically continue for four to six rounds, until the coachee and coach feel that the new approach has been mastered.

Again, staff can only really cope with coaching on one area at a time, possibly two or three in total in a school year. This means that we have to, again, be highly selective in deciding which initiatives to prioritise through this approach.

Maintain previously introduced practice through weekly 'ward-rounds'

As a leader, you and your leadership team will want to 'take the temperature' on the quality of teaching and learning across the school regularly. We have all fallen into the trap of introducing a new approach, intensively monitoring it for the first year, seeing it has been embedded and then never going back to look at it again. We then proudly tell an inspector or other visitor how well embedded this technique is only to find that, over a period of time, it has mutated and degraded to the point where all consistency and efficacy is lost.

The hard truth is that no matter how good the original training and coaching was, without regular 'check-ups', all whole school approaches will start to fail.

And this is where the regular weekly ward round can check the health of teaching in any particular subject or area. Again, this is not about blame or 'catching people out'. It is best to simply be honest and explain that natural degradation of an approach will happen naturally over time and that this is the way to keep all practice sharp.

A ward round is just another form of learning walk. It involves leaders popping into every class and spending five minutes 'taking the temperature' of a particular subject or initiative. It is focused on information gathering and not specific teachers. Most of the time no individual feedback will be given at all, although there will usually be either a discussion at staff meeting about what is working well and what can be sharpened up, or a simple email to all staff with any whole-school action points to consider.

Initially staff were suspicious of leaders observing them so often, but we explain that we are not observing how well individual teachers are performing, but how well school systems are performing. These days, staff barely notice our presence as it has become just 'what we do here'. Alongside regular pupil conferencing and 'book looks' (ideally carried out as part of a pupil conference as the books alone are but a shadow of what was actually learnt), ward rounds are one of the most useful 'low threat, high impact' strategies the leader has for knowing what is going on in the classrooms.

Headteachers should teach

Not every day – but sometimes.

Your title is again a clue and I believe that a headteacher who still teaches from time to time sends out a powerful message to the staff, to the children and to the parents.

It shows that you still have 'skin in the game'; that you can still do the thing that you are asking staff to do. Even as an executive headteacher, I still teach regularly and coach the school's Athletics Club every Thursday after school (nothing gets in the way of this).

A headteacher who teaches is likely to be more curious about teaching and will have a sense of what it is like for the rest of the team.

Headteachers should plan

Again, not every week – but sometimes.

When we asked subject leaders to create skeleton plans for all classes, we allocated each senior leader a subject leader to support and mentor. We physically sat with them and helped them plan these units. Not every time, and not for the whole session, but we were present and interested.

This helped us understand what the subject leader was trying to achieve and gave us an 'in' if we had questions or wanted to check on why a decision was made. And it gave us as leaders' insight to the irritants and wrinkles in the planning process which needed to be ironed out.

And the subject leaders enjoyed us taking this interest. They liked it still more when it became clear that they knew far more than we did and had to explain a planning decision much like a child explaining how to use the Sky remote to an elderly parent.

Headteachers should attend training

This final point should again be obvious, but I have seen headteachers, particularly very senior and experienced headteachers, suddenly find important tasks which need to be done in their office whilst the teachers are learning how to teach phonics etc.

This sets a terrible example. It says to staff that we have lost interest in teaching and no longer feel the need to keep up to date. It also makes it virtually impossible to coach staff or monitor how effective a new approach has been implemented across the school.

So, sit in every staff meeting and every INSET and learn what the staff learn. Your emails can wait.

Key takeaways

1. Make sure staff understand the 'why' of a new initiative or approach, including how it aligns with the school's vision.

2. Create Research & Development teams to trial new approaches prior to whole-school roll-out.

3. Keep the main thing the main thing (in terms of the amount of training time given to priorities).

4. Codify new approaches so that staff can learn to master each step.

5. Use instructional coaching to support staff in mastering new approaches.

Reflection tasks

Consider a new teaching initiative which you are planning to introduce.

Can you articulate the 'why'? How does it align with the school's vision?

_____

_____

_____

_____

_____

What evidence do you have that it is solving a problem which needs to be solved?

_____

_____

_____

_____

_____

What time and resources have you made available to prepare for this change (prior to the training itself)?

_____

_____

_____

_____

_____

How will you codify the new approach and break it down into a teaching routine?

_____

_____

_____

_____

_____

How will you sequence staff training to ensure that they can master the new initiative a step at a time? How are training sessions spaced across the term/ year?

_____

_____

_____

_____

_____

How will you organise Instructional Coaching to ensure that staff are supported to embed the new approach?

_____

_____

_____

_____

_____

How will you as leader monitor teaching and learning to ensure that the approach is embedded (and stays embedded)?

_____

_____

_____

_____

_____

Chapter 7

Spotting systemic problems

Or, a case study on how to fail

I'd felt physically sick for the last 48 hours.

The leadership team and Year 6 teachers sat in my office whilst my Head of School grappled with the DfE's Assessment Portal.

Whilst the reason for feeling like I was about to throw up was daft (we can argue about the whys and wherefores on that one another day), the thought that I would know the outcome of four years of work in a matter of minutes played constantly on my mind.

Today was D-day for an improvement strategy, five years in the making. The moment when I'd learn whether we'd turned a corner or... well... failed.

Again.

I had been headteacher at Blackhorse for over a decade. I had taken it from the bottom of the league tables to, by 2015, near the top. We took these results for granted... we were Blackhorse and (despite some of the highest numbers of SEND pupils in the LA) we knocked out excellent results year after year.

Until we didn't.

A case study of failure

I have spent a great deal of time reflecting on this failure, by way of faltering SATs outcomes in KS2, which caused me so many sleepless nights over a five year period.

As a HT with a reputation for school improvement, they were at first my irritation, then my embarrassment, then my cause for alarm.

Although it sounds hyperbolic: I carried them around with me every day. And whilst I always hoped that other strengths within the school would carry us through our next inspection, the monkey on my back forever whispered catastrophic scenarios in my ears of inspectors pulling the school into Ofsted purgatory.

I have also learned a lot about school improvement.

Whilst the previous chapters have focused on practical tips to drive school improvement forward, this one is a little different.

You see, when discussing school improvement, there is a temptation to 'edit out' the bits which don't fit with a certain narrative (in this case of an all-wise, all-knowing leader). The mythology becomes a sanitised version of the journey, where all your decisions were right and all your actions were pure. These versions of school improvement contain no uncertainty, only the inevitable success of a masterfully crafted plan.

But school improvement isn't like that.

It is messy. It is uncertain. It doesn't always go the way you want.

I believe I have learnt more about school improvement from my difficult failures than from my easy successes.

Here is what I learnt along the way.

Stumble and fall

You must look for early warning signs of decline.

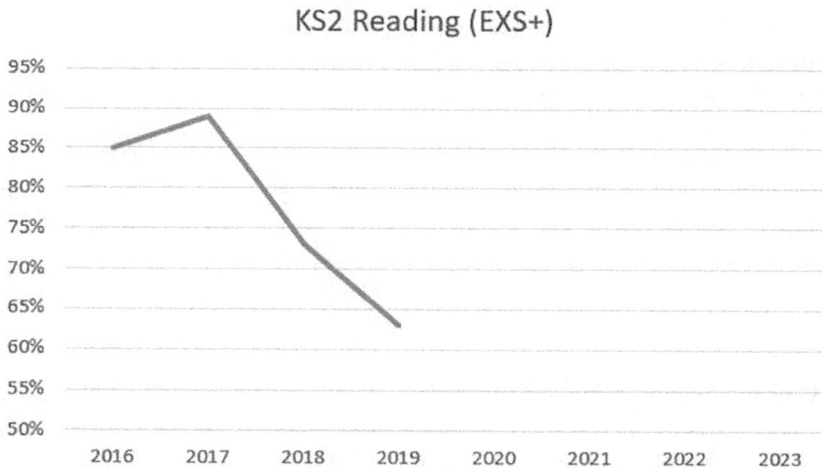

KS2 Reading (EXS+)

Having become accustomed to data 'beginning with a nine' in the old test regime between 2012 and 2015, in 2016, the children at Blackhorse did well when faced with the new tougher-style SATs. In 2017 better again. We (rightly) understood that good SATs scores, whilst not the sole measure of a school, are (as they always were) an important guide to how effective we were as a school.

Then in 2018 the KS2 reading data fell significantly by 15%. One year's data needs to be treated with caution – so much of it can be cohort-specific and gives little true insight into the quality of teaching across the school as a whole. It is also an echo of past teaching – baked in sometimes years before – showing only how a specific cohort performed given the teaching and circumstances which characterised their journey through the school.

However, this excuse cuts both ways. In 2018, having got used to knocking out great outcomes year-on-year, we were too quick to ascribe this to 'bad luck' and didn't take this first opportunity to look forensically at the reasons for this sudden decline. We instead created detailed excuses at a pupil level for why this child or that had underperformed.

In July 2019 we once again downloaded our data to discover that reading had dropped to 63% EXS (a drop of 30% on two years earlier).

It would be wrong to say we did nothing strategically to improve outcomes in reading during these first two years of decline – it is just that we would later learn that, in the absence of any meaningful understanding of the nature of the problem, we enacted the wrong solution.

One year is bad luck, two years is a worry… three years is a trend… a trend and, as head, my responsibility.

Pride (and a lack of understanding teaching efficacy) comes before a fall

I am increasingly of the opinion that the most dangerous moment for any successful school is the year after a successful Ofsted inspection.

I am also of the opinion that the second most dangerous moment for any successful school is following a run of good results.

In my first five years at Blackhorse, the staff had vivid memories of being at the bottom of the heap, trying to claw their way up. They remembered the countless LA 'Teaching and Learning Reviews'; the uncertain future where the school had no past glories in the community bank.

Yet by 2016, those memories had faded, replaced by a narrative which saw Blackhorse soaring ever higher (much like Icarus). The team (spurred on by me) saw only blue skies ahead… we weren't any school – we were Blackhorse – and were therefore slow to act when the facts started to tell a different story.

And whilst we had spent a lot of time re-designing our teaching approaches in maths and writing, following the need to improve outcomes, we had not looked at reading in the same forensic detail. Results had always been good so we 'left it alone' and were therefore unclear as to which parts of our reading recipe actually worked and which parts didn't. So when results took a tumble, we were left scratching our heads.

Be dispassionate about your teaching approaches

Many of us will be familiar with 'sunk cost fallacy': 'the phenomenon whereby a person is reluctant to abandon a strategy or course of action because they have invested heavily in it, even when it is clear that abandonment would be more beneficial'.

In 2018 Ofsted saw the dip in reading scores and prescribed a focus on comprehension in reading in their 'next steps'. If I'm honest, this was just parroting what we'd told them, having already implemented a new approach which saw children spending up to an hour a day on reading comprehension.

This for us was 'job done'. We'd diagnosed the problem (albeit superficially and – as we'd later discover – wrongly) and had put in a fix which mirrored what most schools around us were doing: a daily diet of focused, domain-specific, written comprehension questions.

Surely five hours a week of focused comprehension would sort out the problem?

We sat for a good 18 months before the data showed us that the cost (in terms of teacher planning hours and curriculum time) had warranted virtually no improvement in outcomes.

What we should have done was rigorously, systematically and (above all) dispassionately evaluate this chosen approach to uncover whether it was actually working.

We didn't do that.

But before we move on, let's hear from another talented school leader who had to unpick failure…

Case Study: Ro O'Reilly

Headteacher at St Nicholas Chantry Primary School, Evidence Leader in Education for the Somerset Research School

On the day of my interview for Headship at St Nick's, I witnessed the most dangerous and chaotic Art lesson I'd ever seen… and the children were only painting. It left me feeling queasy. Some classrooms had broken windows, and clutter was everywhere. Yet, something about the school drew me in – it reminded me of my own primary school. The staff were so kind and welcoming, and the children were friendly and articulate; I couldn't wait to get started.

Just before I took up headship of St. Nicks, Ofsted called, and the school narrowly escaped an 'inadequate' judgment. Staff morale was at an all-time low. This was the second RI judgment here. St. Nick's was my third headship, and I knew I could make a difference, as I had at my previous schools, both of which had also faced significant issues. When asked by a governor about my 'formula' for school improvement, I replied: 'hard work and honesty'. I wouldn't change this response, although we all know there is much more to it than this. However, as the daughter of a deputy head and a farmer, hard work is ingrained in me, as well as absolute transparency.

Despite being a lovely place with decent results, St Nick's was not thriving. There were pockets of exemplary practice, but not enough of them. Where practice was worst, this was not addressed or supported, so staff were working blind. The curriculum and environment needed vast improvement. The leadership team lacked clarity, self-belief and the autonomy to grow; preventing staff and pupils from reaching their potential. Two years later, leaders are flourishing. Most have stayed, helping to transform the school, while new recruits bring fresh perspectives and energy.

Revamping the environment was a significant task. Every room and shared area was cluttered. We stripped everything back to reveal the very best of our beautiful, historic school. Some staff were brave enough to admit this was not for them and they moved on. I promised those who stayed it would be worth it. Most did, and they've found the hard work incredibly rewarding. Our Trust, Futura, helped update neglected classrooms with new technology, and we established consistency in displays, ensuring classrooms were beautiful and belonged to the children, supporting learning and everyone's mental health.

Our stunning school site, with views from Clevedon to the Mendips, had never involved children in decisions about its design for high-quality play. This led to unkind, unsafe behaviour at playtimes, spilling into classrooms. I prioritised pupil leadership and pupil voice, which has become a strength of St Nick's. Students now design outdoor spaces. We are now an OPAL school with enhanced play areas (giant sand pit, digging pit with real spades, giant loose parts to name just some of the fun). OPAL Play leaders and Pupil Chaplains are on hand to support play and any issues arising. Play opportunities designed by our children have led to them being happier and having their needs met. Parents applaud and appreciate these changes, despite the occasional grumble about muddy clothes.

Engaging parents and carers has been the biggest challenge of all. After years of feeling and hearing that their child's school was not good enough, building trust has taken time, patience and energy. We now make more regular opportunities to invite parents in for tours and coffee mornings. I am always on the gate, rain or shine to welcome and listen. I always try to own any issues raised rather than become defensive. Listening to parents without preconception has been crucial, because they always, without exception have a point we can learn and grow from. Occasionally meeting families in their own home has been vital in mending bridges.

As I examined the curriculum, I found it hastily borrowed and lacking precision. Leaders struggled with its application, leading to inconsistent retention of skills and knowledge. It certainly wasn't an inclusive curriculum, with too many pupils withdrawn for ineffective interventions. We have now adopted our Trust's ambitious curriculum, improving understanding and application, resulting in better pupil outcomes and engagement. Leaders and teachers have worked hard to make this curriculum right for St Nick's with a real drive on experiential learning and using our incredible local area whenever we can. Pupils with SEND have their needs met via expert-led CPD for staff and better, smarter IEPs with support, wherever possible, happening as part of high-quality teaching. Pupils with SEND have their own Neurodiversity Champions' leadership group, and they, as well as disadvantaged learners are proportionately represented in all our pupil leadership groups.

Leading St Nick's is challenging but incredibly rewarding. Being comfortable driving improvement with initially egg-shaped wheels, is a skill in itself, requiring patience, humour and endless, genuine optimism. Addressing root problems in granular detail has been vital for our transformation. Openness has built trust within the community, and I always, without exception prioritise the children. I own my mistakes and apologise for these. Heads are only human after all. I aim for excellence, not perfection in myself and others. One of my mantras has always been 'If it's good enough for my child, it's good enough for any child'. Using this with staff has helped them see their practices through the lens of a child and certainly led to improvements in practice. Knowing we have the support of our Trust has helped so much – this wider team is such a blessing and a huge part of who we are today.

Two years on, St Nick's past inadequacies are behind us. We've had excellent outcomes in recent SIAMS and Ofsted inspections, lifting the previous cloud of doom and insecurity for everyone. However, the day after the great inspection outcome, fresh challenges remain and the blocked drain still needs dealing with. The difference is that our school has a renewed spirit and energy, thanks to everyone's hard work and honesty, and I couldn't be prouder of St Nick's. Our school motto – 'Be a Good Shepherd' can be seen through everyone's care for one another and our environment; it's simply a wonderful place to belong.

Ro provides a great example of leveraging leadership from all parts of the community to drive school improvement, which we can all learn from.

Now back to Blackhorse's reading conundrum…

Be 'evidence-informed'

The term 'evidence-informed' is used to justify almost every teaching initiative at the moment. It is the buzz-word that guarantees success.

But few of us delve any deeper and ask 'where is this evidence from?' or 'can this evidence be trusted?' The school's tilt towards hours and hours of comprehension practice was in our minds 'evidence-informed' – in so much as it was what a lot of other schools were doing and quite a few advisers talked about it enthusiastically. This resulted in us not doing any actual research on reading approaches for ourselves – instead we succumbed to 'group think' with the schools around us. Interestingly, as previously mentioned, Ofsted validated our chosen solution in their 2018 report. It appears that even the inspectorate aren't immune to the echo chamber.

The second issue with 'evidence-informed practice' is that we tend to apply it more to external approaches, which we seek to adopt, and less to examining what is actually happening in our own classrooms.

At the time, we had almost no evidence as to what was going on in terms of children's mastery of reading beyond comprehension test scores. This meant that we knew only the crude output data and had no understanding of its relationship to the various inputs (the teaching strategies). Moreover, because we were measuring the short-term success of these strategies against how closely staff were following these prescribed approaches, we weren't measuring impact on learning, but impact on teaching, providing a false sense of success.

In short, the evidence base for our chosen solution was weak and we didn't think to challenge the orthodoxy of those around us.

Your improvement strategy is only as good as the data you collect

In order to truly understand a problem, and then understand whether your chosen 'best bet' is having impact, you need 'three-dimensional' data.

Part of our issue was that we didn't really have enough data available to show us where the actual problem with our teaching approach lay. We had comprehension test data, and phonics scores, but nothing else. Our understanding of the problem was therefore one dimensional, resulting in misdiagnosis and time and effort being wasted on the wrong thing.

We had assumed that children were getting low scores on comprehension tests because we weren't teaching comprehension well enough. We were further distracted by lesson observations which indicated that staff were teaching comprehension well, but again, we were falling into the trap of evaluating teaching instead of evaluating learning.

We were distracted still further by data for Years 3-5 looking strong, only to come out weak in Year 6 SATs, not noticing that *how* tests were being administered left the clue which would eventually solve the riddle.

This was because we weren't collecting data which would help us diagnose the problem.

Which left us guessing.

It would take us another year before we started to collect more 'three-dimensional' data on reading which included individual phonics decoding, reading speed, a prosody rubric, vocabulary checks and then… and only then… comprehension.

Stop and think!

The English educational leadership disease is that of 'always doing'.

Activity is often more highly valued than impact. Pace of activity is our opium, as it provides a reassuring narrative of progress. It is supported by a plot within inspection reports which praises rapidity and chides sluggishness.

It wasn't until we'd repeatedly failed that we decided that we couldn't keep looking for the magic bullet which would signal our salvation.

So, well into our fourth year of reading results failure, we stopped to think. We spent the first four months of the annual School Development Plan… well… thinking. Researching the problem. Reading around the subject to gain more insight into how a child's reading journey progressed.

In a system which appears to reward activity over impact ('I must show the inspector that I've been taking rapid steps to resolve the issues'), this felt worryingly slow.

We systematically and dispassionately interrogated the school's system for the teaching of reading. We compared this with the 'best bets' available through the (sometimes thin) published research.

We worked hard again to improve our provision and, again, when tests returned in 2022, saw a modest rise, although still well below even the first drop in 2018.

KS2 Reading (EXS+)

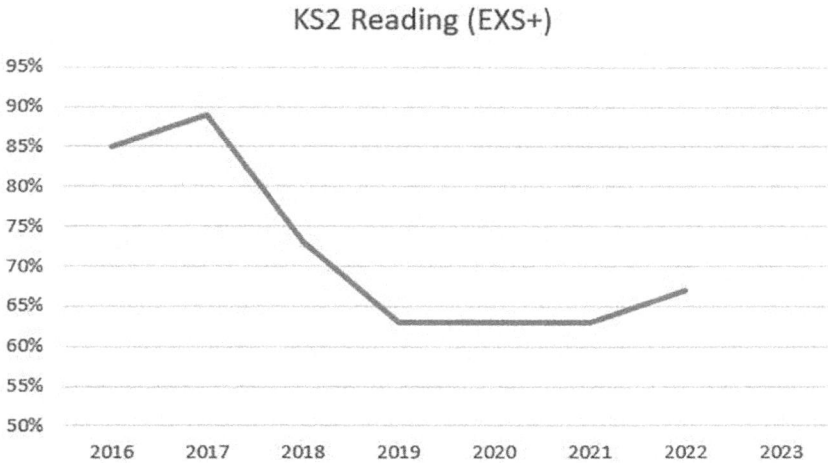

Another huge issue in many primary schools is that middle leaders are often over-stretched and have limited non-contact time. As we've discussed previously, thinking time isn't prioritised.

This often results in a drive to monitor simple compliance, with time-pressed leaders judging the success of an initiative based purely on whether simple and easy-to-observe surface-level features are being adhered to. Once again, analytical thinking time is de-prioritised in the drive to show that you're using your one afternoon of non-contact effectively (and by effectively I mean by looking busy). Worst still, the leader, knackered from a full-time class commitment, having done a brief compliance check, hides in their office making tables to email out to staff.

We were fortunate to have sufficient financial reserves to afford to give some middle leaders a day or more out of class a week. This made a huge difference as for the first time they had the capacity and head space to truly examine the problem.

This is where the messiness of school improvement doesn't sit with our desire for a linear narrative where a problem is encountered, is briefly grappled with, and then promptly overcome. Even with this renewed focus and more data, the solution didn't fall into our laps right away. Endless school improvement tales reinforce this myth with stories of a wise leader waltzing in, immediately happening upon the solution and finishing the school year with tea and medals.

The truth is that sometimes, the solution doesn't present itself straight away.

By 2022, reading had been the number one priority on every School Development Plan since 2019. So in the autumn of 2022, we paused again. We read some more and, most importantly, we analysed the now more three-dimensional data we had on reading.

And it was this that lead to the breakthrough.

Once you have good evidence/ data – analyse it forensically

Having started collecting much more granular information about how children were decoding and comprehending in the important middle primary years (Years 3-4), we discovered that children could decode (phonics scores were always high), but they weren't developing the fluency needed to read quickly and with meaning.

Moreover, when we then went back to look at the teaching of reading comprehension, we discovered our system of teaching resulted in the teacher often reading a text to the children and not expecting them to read it for themselves.

Exploring the interconnection between teaching (input) and learning (output), we made a breakthrough. Busy teachers were skating over the reading part of the comprehension lesson, reading far too much of a text to the children instead of with the children. As a result, children weren't achieving enough 'reading miles' (time spent individually reading) to read at a speed and accuracy which was quick enough. Moreover, teachers, whilst well-meaning, would often tag on an extra ten minutes to formal reading comprehension tests, further masking the problem of slow reading and limited fluency in the internal data. It was therefore only in Year 6, with more rigid assessment timings, that the problem manifested itself.

Now we look for 'best bets'

Once reading fluency had been identified as a hypothetical cause for our reading standards problem at KS2, we again committed to look at the research and identify some 'best bets'.

The EEF and DfE's Reading Framework (latest version, 2023) provided research which appeared to back our hypothesis, and we settled on a focus on fluency and vocabulary building. But again, we spent the first three months of the year deciding on which strategies to follow.

During this time we looked at how other successful schools had operationalised fluency practice in reading. We also got in touch with reading expert Chris Such, who generously helped us to break fluency teaching down into a teachable, observable approach.

Slow down to speed up!

Whilst, with Ofsted at the gates, the temptation would have been to rush out half-baked fluency approaches with limited training, this time we went really slowly. We spent a year introducing just three approaches, spending dozens of staff meetings training staff, with fortnightly low-threat instructional coaching so that we could master each element as a team before moving on to the next.

The result? Change that was deeply understood and embedded.

Codify once all the kinks have been smoothed out

Again, the temptation is always to present staff at INSET with a fully finished article for fear of looking foolish if something doesn't work perfectly first time. However, whilst the core of the approaches had been nailed down fully before training, we spent the year hammering out the kinks and making sure every element ran efficiently.

Only then did we publish fully our complete strategy – printed professionally to give value to the hundreds of hours of research, disappointments and practice which had led us to a level of understanding.

*

Five years of living dangerously

'I'm in!' declared my Head of School, having spent 20 minutes trying to access the assessment portal.

Looking across at the assembled Year 6 team, more than one of them looked as sick as I did.

'Okay Sadie first, could be a bit cuspy... 105.'

It was a good start.

'Isla... 119.'

'Mohammed... 108.'

Within the first five results we knew something had shifted. Children were scoring well into, or exceeding, their predicted levels, instead of scraping through (or not), which had become the norm.

What's more, the maths results had also jumped. Most children had met or exceeded their targets, with 83% of children achieving the expected standard, irrespective of the 15% of children in the cohort with EHCPs.

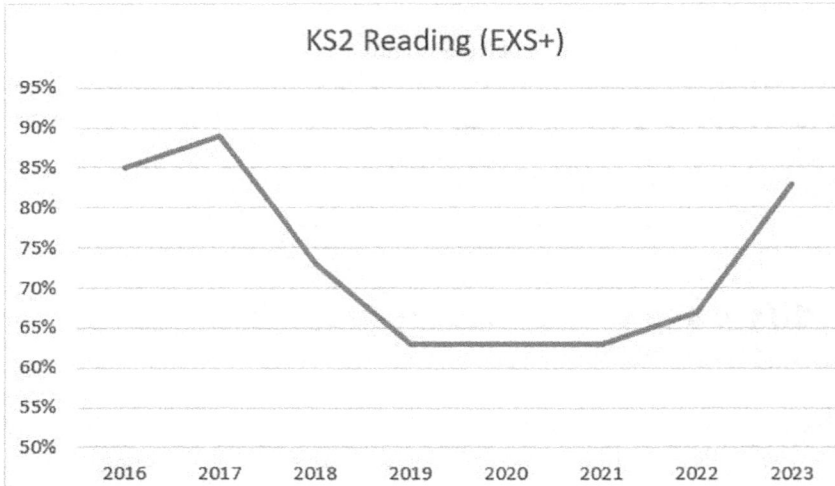

KS2 Reading (EXS+)

It took every fibre of my being not to burst into tears (unlike two of the Year 6 team who wept openly).

At time of writing, the reading results have continued on an upward trajectory. And whilst I wear the monkey's scars on my back forever more, I do believe that the experience of failing taught me a great deal as a headteacher.

And so, if you are grappling with thorny standard issues, take heart – and take note. There is no magic bullet, no hastily enacted cure. But there is a process which, if you follow it, and then hold the course throughout the inevitable setbacks and disappointments, you will eventually see those green shoots of improvement.

And if you are flying high on great results then long may it continue.

But keep your feet on the ground.

*

Key takeaways

1. Ensure that you have sufficiently rigorous data to assess the efficacy of whole school teaching approaches.

2. Always be on the lookout for early signs of declining standards.

3. Be dispassionate in evaluating the effectiveness of whole-school teaching approaches.

4. Take your time in examining the problem, and then researching and trialling possible new approaches.

5. Research evidence needs to be examined thoroughly alongside the context of the school.

Reflection tasks

Which areas of practice within your school are showing early warning signs of declining standards? How do you know?

_____

_____

_____

_____

_____

Pick one area of your school's practice which you are unhappy with. List all of the outcomes (in terms of data and pupil learning) and then all of the inputs (in terms of curriculum and teaching approaches). Which of the inputs is negatively impacting on the outcomes?

_____

_____

_____

_____

_____

Look at your current School Development Plan. How much research and reflection time is built into adopting a new teaching approach? Do leaders have sufficient time to complete this research and trial new approaches or are new initiatives rushed in?

_____

_____

_____

_____

_____

Chapter 8

Creating a happy and effective staff team

Encouraging the team to follow you

'I'm going back…We need to discuss what happened!'

I sat in the training room, looking out at a cold grey carpark and fumed.

'It's a terrible idea, Simon – don't do it!' protested my deputy.

It was the day after the LA's 'Teaching and Learning Review'.

The day after the LA's Commissar had made it pretty clear that she expected me to improve teaching at the school. And fast… if I wanted to continue my fledgling career as a headteacher.

I had been at some training or other for the day, along with the deputy, so hadn't had time to feed back to the staff on how the review had gone. Or rather, how badly it had gone. It was staff meeting night, so (as the course was wrapping up) I had time to head back to school for a post-mortem.

'It's like they'd forgotten all the things we worked on!' I hissed.

'Go home – whatever you say tonight will come out wrong and could do more harm than good!'

I paused. I knew she was right. Trust is built over months and years and can be lost in an instant.

'No… I'm going back!'

I picked up my coat and headed back to school.

The staff meeting was a disaster.

*

I have worked in a number of staff teams during my time before headship. One or two have been tight and focused, working towards a single goal, which seemed joyful, no matter how hard the work, as we all felt deeply committed to the school and what it was trying to achieve. I never worried about my wellbeing and gave freely of my time because I loved my job. I learnt a huge amount at these places and leaving was a wrench.

Some were 'fine', effective but lacking in any passion or 'spark'. I may have grown professionally at these places, but I never felt any real connection or loyalty. I occasionally grumbled about my wellbeing at these places as everything seemed somewhat 'transactional'. I quickly moved on from these schools when the next opportunity came into view.

One was a car crash, with weak and inept leadership leaving a vacuum to be filled by infighting, factionalism and, ultimately, failure. Wellbeing was reduced to survival – to getting through each day without too much drama. As (at the time) a relatively inexperienced member of staff without any leadership responsibility, I initially believed that if I worked harder and better, this school would improve. It didn't and I eventually left.

All of us who have spent any time in any team, be it in education or elsewhere, will recognise these three descriptions. Most of us have probably worked in all three.

The interplay between people and place and effort and meaning is the riddle which we must all solve if we are to create effective and happy teams. And as such, these will be the themes explored in this chapter.

'Wellbeing' will be weaved through – good staff wellbeing is essential to any healthy team – but I won't be talking about buying doughnuts every Friday (although who doesn't like a doughnut on a Friday), or paying for a head massage (as one head I worked for did – which was lovely – only they forgot about the TAs or admin staff – which naturally didn't go down well). There are numerous tips and hacks and genuinely lovely ideas which get floated all the time regarding wellbeing, but I won't be discussing these. Not because they aren't important, or that they can sometimes oil the wheels, but because I believe that effective and happy teams are built on something deeper.

'Don't be evil'

'Don't be evil' was Google's slogan until 2015, when it was changed to 'do the right thing'.

One might wonder why a company needs to remind itself not to be evil, as it suggests that the temptation to be evil was something it was always grappling with. However, they were right to put this at the start of their code of conduct as building a great team starts with the behaviour of the leaders.

I have seen truly appalling leadership behaviours by some stratospherically successful headteachers. I know of one (who will remain nameless) who told a member of (my) staff looking round for a job that 'I expect my staff to work 364 days of the year – Christmas day is yours'. Their school was rated 'outstanding', had amazing outcomes and they were heralded as a brilliant leader by the Great and the Good.

However, they are (objectively) a terrible human being.

Invariably, these leaders' 'win at all costs' mentality results in them burning through staff at a rate of knots until even the glitz and glamour of a flagship school is enough to attract and retain good people.

And whilst this is an extreme example, as leaders, we must all check our behaviours all the time. If we are to truly inspire the loyalty of our team then we must practise what we preach and live the values of our school.

Moreover, we must see our staff first as human beings, and then within their role. We must make the effort to know the big things going on in their lives, the names of their kids, how their elderly mother is doing. A moment's check-in with a team member as you walk about the school, asking about these things, makes a big difference to the individual, and trickles down through the team.

In short, as leaders, we must be seen to always be kind and never be evil.

'The best organisations behave like a cult'

…at least to begin with.

This may seem like a strange (and potentially dangerous) suggestion. However, hear me out…

Steven Bartlett (2023), when analysing what successful organisations had in common, concluded that all of them, at the beginning at least, behaved in many respects like a cult. He described the key ingredients of both cults and effective and dynamic businesses as having the following:

1. a shared mission;
2. a sense of community and belonging;
3. an inspirational leader;
4. an 'us and them' mentality.

Now this cocktail could very easily become a toxic brew whereby a power-crazed leader creates a deeply unhealthy workplace. Indeed, I've seen schools which go on to fail spectacularly adopt many, if not all, of these ingredients.

However, if carried through sensibly and thoughtfully, I believe that there is some wisdom here.

A strong shared vision and mission – as we've discussed throughout – is essential in building that sense of community and belonging, as well as setting the culture of the team. Daniel Pink (2010), describes 'Purpose' as one of the three main drivers of intrinsic motivation (alongside autonomy and mastery). If we believe in the purpose, the vision of our school, then we are more likely to feel a sense of belonging and community.

An inspirational leader is also, I believe, essential. That said, I also believe that inspirational leaders come in all shapes and sizes; you don't have to be loud and bombastic to fill this description. I have known many quiet and unassuming school leaders who demand just as much respect as those who are more extroverted. People follow leaders, not committees. So, as headteacher, you need to inspire those you work with through your passion and your actions and your behaviours.

As for the 'them and us' mentality, this is probably the most difficult to do with grace. As I have described previously, I have worked with deeply partisan leaders who would create a 'cult of exceptionalism' and I loved the 'pride in the badge' which they inspired from me. I would almost certainly be described as one such leader myself and will passionately defend and promote the schools which I lead. However, I have also seen this used as the last refuge of the scoundrel – creating a bunker mentality when things are going wrong and blaming external forces for every problem. Use the 'us' to describe how you believe your school is different and special by all means, but avoid the degradation of others in the 'them'.

Tell stories and share successes

This is really a no-brainer, but often we British feel coy about talking up our successes for fear of being labelled vain or boastful. And whilst this can be off-putting to others, particularly if it comes across as bragging on the school's social media feeds, it can be a force for good if done with humility and sensitivity.

As we've previously discussed, stories, which then fade into school mythology over time, reinforce a sense of traction, of moving forward achieving aspects of our mission. During my first headship, when the school was beset with challenges, a staff member told me that they needed to hear me reeling off the week's successes in the Friday assembly as much as the children did.

Publicly celebrating successes which the school has a right to be proud of, big or small, reinforces the narrative that the school is on the right path. Praising staff in staff meetings, deliberately noticing and celebrating their efforts, has a huge impact on both individual and team morale. So too does 'future focused' language when the goal is still a long way off. For example, we constantly talked about 'when we are outstanding' as a team when I was leading schools which were at risk of special measures. And whilst I probably wouldn't give Ofsted so much emphasis in this day and age, at the time it did fix the minds of worried staff on the 'inevitable outcome' to their hard work and teamwork.

First meet people's need for psychological safety

Whilst trust and respect are built brick by brick over months and years (as the team starts to believe that a leader is worthy of their trust and respect as a result of their words, behaviours and actions aligning with the values which they espouse), there are practical actions which leaders can use to address short-term fears which can negatively impact on staff morale.

One of these Brené Brown (2018) describes as 'container building'; in short, defining the psychological boundaries and expectations which the team can expect either in the short or long term. It can start by simply acknowledging fears and worries and validating them as normal, reasonable and expected reactions to something which the mind considers unexpected or threatening. For instance, being told you'll be using a new planning format for reports can, for many, release exactly the same hormones into the bloodstream as when being chased by a lion. It can also make it clear what everyone should expect from one another in terms of behaviours at a single meeting.

Container building also allows the team, led by the leader, to discuss openly the behaviours which each should expect of one another when discussing anything, including topics or initiatives which might be controversial or difficult. By agreeing that 'it's OK to raise concerns freely and give voice to worries' tells the team that there will be no negative consequences for this, also avoiding what Brown describes as the 'dirty yes' – agreeing with something in a staff meeting only to criticise it with your pals in your classroom (behind a closed door) afterwards. 'We will listen to feedback but will have to consider it alongside our desire to improve X', also manages expectations that all feedback will automatically result in changes to the original plan.

Container building can't be tokenistic. You can't ask for people's honest feedback in a meeting and then get cross when they give it to you. Expectations and behaviours on all sides need to be recognised. Something as simple as 'we will be fully present and engaged' can ensure that there's nobody 'opts out' only to criticise later.

But above all container building points at the elephant in the room: that some decisions are fraught with worry and uncertainty (things we as humans don't cope well with). And in my experience, by pointing to the elephant and making it OK for it to be there, it often then disappears.

Rumble with vulnerability

This is another insightful suggestion from Brené Brown, who explains that 'Trust is the stacking and layering of small moments and reciprocal vulnerability over time'. She suggests that it is impossible for team members to feel comfortable displaying vulnerability in front of their leader, unless the leader themselves is modelling this. When I was first a headteacher, a teacher told me that they were impressed that I was as open about what I didn't know as what I did. And yet another staff member described the moment I told the team I was leaving to take up a new headship, through a broken voice (I loved the school I was leaving), as the first time I'd allowed them to see genuine vulnerability. I took this lesson with me to my second headship and endeavoured to come across less like a self-contained automaton.

What 'rumbling with vulnerability' is not, however, is 'over-sharing'. I have sadly seen a great many leaders lose the trust of their team by constantly offloading every worry onto them all of the time. This is not modelling vulnerability but modelling neediness. It's okay to share that a situation is complex or difficult. It is not OK to share that you are scared or out of your depth, except to a tiny few confidants; as showing fear, as opposed to temporary uncertainty, will make others feel that nobody is in control.

Brown describes certain meetings as 'rumbles'. These are meetings which may be difficult or fraught with uncertainty or a lack a clear solution. By acknowledging this with the team, a leader meets the team members as follow human beings, which makes others feel less threatened. Sometimes, as heads, we need to rumble with our teams in order to grapple with difficult problems.

Clear is kind – unclear is unkind

Humans have a habit in talking in riddles. And we British, in our efforts to be polite and 'affable', will often dress up what we are trying to say so much that it becomes impossible for the person to whom we are trying to deliver a difficult message to understand what we actually mean.

Kim Scott lays this problem out in a simple framework (2017).

She asserts that, whilst we think we are being kind in 'sparing someone's feelings' by not directly discussing a difficult or potentially thorny issue, we are often (unwittingly) being unkind by having a 'half-conversation' with them, leaving them feeling uneasy, and, most often, confused.

She describes these 'half-conversations' as either *low* care for the individual and a lack of willingness to challenge directly, which results in 'manipulative insincerity'; or *high* care for the individual and a lack of willingness to challenge directly, resulting in 'ruinous empathy'. Sadly, I see these two outcomes often (and have been guilty of creating them myself). Kim Scott suggests that kind and effective communication is the result of high personal care for the individual and a willingness to challenge directly. This is difficult and takes some practice as it goes against many of our cultural norms in the UK. However, I have found that it results in much better communication, with both people in the conversation feeling comfortable to say what they are actually thinking and, most importantly, concluding the conversation with trust and respect intact.

This does not mean, however, that you should constantly speak your mind all of the time. Kim describes a fourth type of conversation where there is low care for the individual (and their feelings), and a high willingness to challenge. She calls this 'obnoxious aggression'. Sadly, I have seen a breed of school leaders behave in an obnoxiously aggressive way towards staff, especially when giving feedback, as they believe that they are 'telling it straight'. These interactions don't anticipate the imbalance of power which is often present, resulting in the leader feeling that they can be direct to the point of rudeness, whilst the team member feels unable give an honest response.

Clear is kind, unclear is unkind. Blunt is just rude.

Ask for regular formal and informal feedback

We as leaders need to know the mood in camp. Whether morale is good, bad or indifferent, unless we have access to this information we are forever working in the dark. So knowing this information is key to an effective and happy staff team.

As we mentioned at the start of the book, in your first 100 days, a cup of tea and an informal chat with each staff member can give a valuable insight into how people are feeling on an individual level. But to understand the team as a whole, you need other mechanisms for gathering this information.

Like most, my schools have 'Staff Wellbeing Teams'. These are made up of representatives of each part of the workforce (office, site, TAs and teachers) who meet termly to discuss ways to make the school a happier, and *more effective* place. It is important to note, that these are *problem-solving* forums, not problem-venting forums. Early on, we had one member of the group come with a long list of petty complaints about anything and everything. It became clear that this staff member wasn't representing their team but was grinding their own axe. However, because the headteacher only attends as another group member, the rest of the group quickly reminded her to come with solutions and the team's behaviour became self-policing. After each meeting minutes are circulated so that everyone can see what has been discussed and decided. And whilst occasionally bigger issues do emerge, these regular, solution-focused, check-ins allow leaders the option of tiny 'course corrections' to initiative roll-outs or other areas which are causing worry. Likewise, it also gives time for the group to discuss why decisions were made. Often, following these discussions, the team concludes that (whilst maybe not popular) the decision made by leaders was, in fact, the right one, which they then relay themselves back to their teams.

The Wellbeing Team also run the anonymous annual staff survey. We tend to use the Ofsted staff survey questions as a basis, with specific questions sometimes added if the team are looking for more information on a particular issue. Having run these surveys for many years over several schools, there is a predictable pattern of the 'marmite responses' within the first twelve hours: two or three staff who love the school, and one or two staff who are really pissed off. It's worth noting that leaders should be informed by such feedback (one unhappy staff member is one more than we'd like) but not directed by a tiny minority or single individual. Very often these people will deploy what Brené Brown refers to as 'the invisible army', by using the phrase 'people are saying' or 'people think' – giving the impression that everyone thinks what this person is saying. Now, that may well be true (and other responses would help you validate this); but, equally likely, it could just be one person wanting to sound like their view is more commonly held. Reflect carefully on such surveys, but don't assume a single comment is indicative of a wider feeling.

Finally, get into the habit of asking your staff to give feedback. Make it clear to them that, whilst you're always happy to listen, you can't always act on it, but that you would like to hear it nonetheless.

Avoid shame and blame

The last twenty years of school accountability measures have been beset by shame and blame.

In the name of this, bodies like Ofsted and the DfE have publicly chastised schools and labelled them as failing. Or, publicly lauded schools and badged them 'outstanding'.

This warped the system.

Headteachers (scared for their own futures) did all they could to avoid Ofsted's wrath, and in so doing created shame and blame cultures of their own, which, in turn, created a compliance culture: 'they can't get me if I did what I was told'. This culture snuffs out any innovation, and levies a high price on perceived failure. Staff stop trying to genuinely improve teaching – as doing anything other the status quo is risky – and become drones, following leaders' commands without question.

Thankfully the days of high stakes lesson observations and punitive appraisal systems have faded.

We are all constantly learning. We are all prone to mistakes when we are learning. As school leaders we must create a culture where imperfection in practice is part of the learning process and is not (as they were once ascribed) a sign of incompetence.

We need to foster a culture in our schools which supports staff to grow – instead of blaming them for not mastering a new approach straight away.

Create a 'thinking' team

Dr Kulvarn Atwal, an executive headteacher in London, outlines in his excellent book *The Thinking School* (2019) how to develop a team which is constantly researching and refining their practice. You may initially feel that adding the task of 'researcher' to the endless tasks teachers have to complete would increase workload and damage morale (certainly not improve it). However, if done well, creating opportunities for staff to engage in the research and design of new practices actually increases engagement, improves motivation and therefore enhances wellbeing.

Following Kulvarn's ideas, several years ago we changed the focus of staff appraisal to 'professional growth projects'. Put simply, over the course of a year, staff work together in teams to research solutions to existing problems or areas of potential improvement. They spend the first two terms reading around the subject at completing background research. In the spring, they trial an aspect in their classes; again, spending time practising and refining the technique through peer observation and discussion. Finally, in the summer terms they create a whole-school approach which has been thoroughly trialled and has had all the rough edges which come with any new initiative knocked off. Their work then becomes a whole-school approach.

Importantly, staff are given time to complete all of these steps within the school day. We do not expect anyone to take research home with them (teachers are busy enough).

The outcome? Well, aside from some great improvements to teaching and learning, the staff feel more in control of their professional learning, having been given autonomy to develop solutions themselves. Initiatives developed in this way are owned by the whole team and therefore the whole team has a stake in its success.

As Daniel Pink, author of *Drive*, notes, 'Control leads to compliance; autonomy leads to engagement' (2010).

We must model wellbeing

As leaders of teams, we need to be better at modelling and promoting work-life balance. We all know of schools where staff are frowned upon for not being at their desks before 8am, or for leaving before 6pm. One school I know expected staff to stay until 7pm every night!

With patterns of work forever shifted post-Covid in the rest of the world outside of teaching, we need to look again at how we support staff to maintain work-life balance during term time. As Brené Brown puts it, *'We have to let go of exhaustion, busyness, and productivity as status symbols and measures of self-worth. We are impressing no one'* (2018).

As the headteacher, it is our job to model and promote this. And I don't mean chipping off early each night and leaving the rest of the staff working away under a mountain of planning and marking (as I've seen some headteachers do). Nor popping out to a 'meeting' and coming back with a new haircut (yes, I've heard of that too). It means modelling working efficiently and well during sensible working hours and then ensuring that the job is not bigger than those hours for anyone in the building. It means trusting people to work at home during their PPA and not expecting them to be in the building ridiculously early or ridiculously late.

Because if we don't, staff will vote with their feet.

*

Back to 'that' staff meeting

I called the meeting to order and began to ruminate about all that had gone wrong in the LA's Teaching and Learning Review the previous day.

What followed was the most exhausting and demoralising hour of my life.

There were tears... occasional shouting (although not by me)... more tears... and painful silences.

I finished the meeting no closer to unearthing the source of our failure, but in opening this fresh wound with no plan on how to address it, I managed to sap morale and burn through what good will I'd banked in the previous eight months as headteacher. And whilst I 'thought' I'd avoided blame and shame, both hung heavy in the air having escaped between my words in my body language and intonation. Instead of protecting the team from the pressure from on high that I was feeling, I simply pushed it down on top of an already skittish team who had no personal agency to solve whole-school problems alone.

'I think I've messed up,' I confided in my deputy the following day.

'Oh, you have!' she replied cheerily, 'but they've forgiven you.'

'How do I put it right?'

'Well, I've spoken to the team and they think chocolate will do it... Thorntons or such like... nothing cheap!'

I bought the biggest box I could find and left it in the staffroom with a note.

The team forgave me.

I guess chocolates and cake are the key to staff wellbeing after all.

*

Case Study: Dr Vic Carr

Headteacher of Woodlands Primary School, Cheshire, speaker, author of *Leading with Love* and *Authentic School Improvement for Authentic Leaders* and Territorial Army officer

I'm sat in my garden chuckling to myself, not because I've lost my marbles, although to be fair temporary forgetfulness has been an ongoing issue for me for a couple of years now, and I have lost more marbles than I have found (so laughing to myself whilst alone in my garden is not uncommon). Anyway, for context, because it takes ages from the writing to the publishing of a book, it is summer 2024. We broke up yesterday, after my 12th year

---

as an headteacher, after 14 years of enforced austerity, after 28 years in education, and with a new government recently ushered into the halls of power, and for the third year in a row I find myself writing a book (or part of a book)! This time it is for my wonderful friend, Simon, and he has asked me to write about the simple (and not in the slightest bit controversial) topic of 'staffing blunders…'

Safe to say, in the introduction to this chapter I need to be explicit – I can't share names or identify schools where any real-life blunders that I've made, or that other people have made whilst I've been leading them, have happened – not because I'm too proud or too egotistical to expose my own ignorance or stupidity (please see my own books for myriad examples of that!) but because it wouldn't be right to talk about other people and their mistakes without their permission. Many of the blunders I've made involve other people, so I can't really share those. So, what are you reading this for? Well…

What I *am* prepared to do is to share examples of my blunders as a staff member, or broad examples that I've come across over the years, of lessons learned from blunders that I have seen/discussed or supported a whole host of people with – and I will leave the rest to your imagination…

What I do know about mistakes that people make (myself included) is that they are often to do with four different (yet often interlinked) categories: trust, assumption, communication and expectation.

I also know that if you create and maintain a culture as a leader, or if you co-create it as a junior leader or a middle leader, of psychological safety, then you are highly likely to get positive outcomes from *any* mistakes that people make and benefit from lessons that you will undoubtedly *ALL* learn from them. This is preferable to creating a blame culture of toxicity, inherent within which is instability and the resulting serious deterioration of both productivity and staff mental health, not to mention improvement, growth and retention.

I have said before, and I truly believe it, our words matter and as a person with influence they matter even more. This means that what I say I have to believe and also embody in my day-to-day work. Anything I say here, I mean. Anything you say as a school leader with influence will matter, and you should also say what you mean, and mean what you say.

Here goes! There is a great deal of intersectionality about the four categories I referenced earlier, as ever with leadership – how do you separate out one aspect from another? But I have to start somewhere, so let's start with the framework.

Expectations

Prevention is always better than cure. For me, the skeleton, if you like, the almost tangible and perhaps core 'framework' for setting expectations and making them obvious and explicit to all members of the school community is the policies you have. Usually, those policies are informed and agreed by unions, then the government, and finally ratified by governors and shared with staff. In school, policies that relate to staff management, and I do mean 'managing staff', all fall under one real headline which is 'human resource', often called HR for short. But human resource is a vastly complicated topic, and one you would do well to seek advice on if ever in any doubt!

Anyway, the main expectations for staff are set out in the statutory pay and conditions document, issued and updated by the government (2024). The pay policy is what should hopefully protect you as a school leader (particularly once you are in post, you have sight of it and have perhaps agreed it) from making any major staffing blunders that will cost you reputationally and/or financially. If you are reading this and you are *planning* to take on headteacher or principal role, then do make sure that this is one of the very early documents that you are aware of.

Sitting alongside the pay policy (for awareness purposes) are the performance management/appraisal policy, absence management procedure, and the individual's job descriptions (which are invariably extremely explicit about the expectations upon staff members in their roles). If you take over a school and are uncertain what it is exactly that you will be/should be/could be holding a staff member to account for, then their job description is the first place to go. Equally, if you are recruiting as a leader, then be very clear on what you are recruiting *for* because that person specification, and job description, will form the basis of what that staff member, once onboarded, will be expecting to be held accountable for, and what you can then expect to hold them accountable for as well. It really is a two-way process.

When you need to swallow the bitter pill...

I know that there have been times when I have had expectations of staff members which have been far in excess of what they themselves expect because I have not understood their job description or they have not understood it, or they don't have one due to historic management issues. When you have conversations about the discrepancy, it can be awful – depending on your approach, your sophistication (or lack of) in dealing with people, and your experience in having authentic and challenging professional discussion. You may even cause yourself more hassle by wading straight in, rather than taking time to find out and understand... implicit here is the suggestion I would offer that this is exactly what you could do first and foremost on virtually any aspect of school leadership!

Some of the expectations that we have of people are based on heuristics – in our experience, in our worldview, what do we expect of somebody who has a certain number of years of experience to be able to deliver? What do we expect somebody in a certain role to be able to deliver in order to support us, or challenge other staff members, or support and guide children academically? Often, we have to accept that our expectations of ourselves and other people are not always reflected in those held by other people who we work with and lead – either at the time or in the past (which skews their understanding and world view as much as it contradicts yours!). This can cause huge dissonance.

What do I mean? I mean, if we inherit a school and a staff body with a range of personalities of different experiences and different job descriptions/roles/responsibilities and we do not understand them as applied to each individual, and do not take the time to find out, we may expect them to work in a way that we work or have previously had people work with us. We are setting them up to fail in our eyes and theirs if they don't. We may expect them to be able to deliver, and to have been trained in the way that we might have trained them, and that is frankly not always going to be the case. Poor organisational leadership leads to poor management of humans, and a lot of confusion, anxiety and real/perceived failure. If you inherit a school where this has perhaps been the case, then it is even more important to ensure you are clear on expectations.

This broadly segues into the 'assumption' piece, which I will come onto next in more detail, but in assuming that people are as trained as you would expect them to be in any given role, that they understand your values, vision and expectations, you are really setting yourself up for a disappointment and, as stated, that other person for failure.

I wrote in my second book, about school improvement, that assuming people are skilled/qualified/trained and coached to the level that you might ensure somebody is before they were given a responsibility and afterward to ensure they can perform at a high level, is floored. I did it. Cringe. I did it and it cost somebody their peace of mind and confidence for quite some time when they were questioned by an external visitor and could not answer the questions they were being asked. Honestly? That was entirely *my* fault not theirs.

Equally, they clearly did not understand the expectations upon them when they were placed in that role, did not subsequently seek to find out what those expectations might entail in order to be successful, so this is actually a two-way process, and all of us were in some way accountable for that blunder. But as a leader, you should hold yourself to slightly higher standards and simply ensure your expectations are clear, robust, informed and reinforced by policy and correct process and applied with integrity and parity. What I expect, versus what staff expect, is an area of possible conflict. I make sure that we are all clear on this co-constructed reality to prevent conflict, and again this tips over into communication and understanding. As I said earlier, these things are all interlinked and there is great intersectionality between each of the aspects I referenced.

Should you make a blunder as a leader, then please, if I could offer any advice, own it. You cannot hide from a mistake, and you cannot hide it. To do so would be disingenuous and unethical. The best course of action is to own it, apologise for it, understand why it happened, make reparations and take the necessary steps to ensure it does not happen again. Only by doing this do you normalise how to behave after making a mistake.

Assumption

When it comes to assumption, I think I've said it before, my grandfather used to say when you 'assume' anything, it makes an 'ass' of 'u' and 'me'… I will leave that with you.

Often our biases, our heuristics, our life experiences, help our pre-historic brains to save energy and help us to take some shortcuts in our thinking, but do give us pre-conceived ideas without our conscious awareness. Sometimes those ideas become assumptions and they are not always helpful.

When we assume people are like us, and they are not, this can be a big problem. You may not be aware of their divergence initially, or for a while. But it is crucial that you grapple with any deviation from either policy or values immediately and within the framework of your belief system, to reinforce expectations, reinforce the vision of the organisation and the trust that staff have in you as a leader. Where the behaviour or actions of a staff member compromise both policy and values, then it becomes even more important to deal effectively with the issue – as difficult as that sounds.

Confessions of a blunderer

On a smaller, but equally important, scale, some of the blunders I have made in my early career are where I have experienced cognitive dissonance and a degree of frustration and impatience when I think people are as driven, organised, forward thinking, dynamic, committed and relentless as I am told I am, and they are not. With hindsight, and almost 3 decades of experience, it's probably a good thing that they're not any of those things like I am, because everybody I work with would be piling-in and routinely completely burnt out! I realised as a headteacher that I needed people around me who are different to me in the ways they work, but who share the same value set. That is where leadership becomes nuanced. We can learn to work differently, we can adjust and work to the pace and strength of others if we are all self-aware, we can learn to work with more patience, we can learn to take breaks, to work backwards from end state goals, we can look at project management and build in 'air gaps', reflection and additional time for people to learn and grow. We can rarely work towards changing our values. I would say that the biggest staff blunder I made in terms of assumption in the very, very early days was not doing this, and being unaware that staff were trying to keep up with my work ethic, as I was a role model and was unaware of the impact of this, and it was making people burn out and pretty unhappy. Silly billy that I am!

Self-awareness is the key leadership trait here, I think. If you know your own way of working and the expectations you place on yourself, and you are honest about them, then you can begin to understand how they may look to other people, and how they may influence other people and impact on them, and so on. You are the Head or the Principal, which means you have to demonstrate healthy ways of working at all times. Naturally, at times, there are inconsistencies, and the balance may be out. Again, I've been quoted as saying this about myself in the school where I work now. For me, now, it's about knowing when that balance is out because I recognise the signs, articulating and explaining to other people that I know, and then addressing it, for myself and anyone else who is struggling. This has given other people agency and license to do the same thing, and definitely to speak up when they are feeling it and I may be unaware. It means that staff understand that at times they can be extremely busy and the tempo of work is extreme, but that this is not sustainable. Modelling at all times is important as a leader.

I suppose on a personal level, rather than with staff members, not doing this was brought home most acutely to me when I was getting a divorce – during my very first headship. I had only been a headteacher a few months and the divorce unfolded. I tried to be strong for my children, I did all my tear shedding out of their view (in the shower, or when they had gone to bed) and I was upbeat and positive with them the rest of the time. One day my son was extremely upset with me. He was upset about the divorce, naturally, but he challenged me and accused me of *not* being upset, of *not* caring! I was shocked because, of course, I cared very deeply, and I was extremely upset, but his elaboration was that my children had observed that I didn't cry, I hadn't cried as they had, I wasn't visibly upset. So, I quickly learned to express my humanity, to cry when I was sad. I learned to tell them that I was crying because I was sad but that there were things I knew I could do to help myself move on from that sadness and not let it consume me. They learned the language and the strategies of healing as I modelled them.

I translated that way of working into my workplace. It works.

Trust

This is such a huge part of what we do, as leaders, and is both our greatest strength and our most vulnerable weakness. If trust is lost or broken, it is almost impossible to mend. Mutual trust in your school family means your staff will enjoy a culture of psychological safety, and mutual respect, where they know and understand healthy boundaries, can make mistakes and can make reparations in a learning space. Trust in a school, when framed like this, matters because it is also what we are duty bound to model to children and parents by extension.

Moreover, having a culture where trust is prevalent ensures that staff feel secure which will influence stability and reduce turnover – and in a world of recruitment issues, this is fundamental to your school success. By creating a trusting environment, you are also building a diverse and inclusive culture where staff will likely feel a greater sense of belonging and connection to the team, no matter what the external pressures are (looking forward, this may not involve Ofsted for much longer, but we live in hope!). Right now, for example, there is a period of huge change coming in education, and in the UK in general, and that can derail people, none of us like uncertainty. In a supportive environment, created and maintained based on trust (and the elements to do this I will cover below) then minimising amygdala hijack, and anxiety-based responses to change, is much easier for a leader.

Communication

Let's get to know one another…

You might be the most socially awkward and anti-social person that you know (or that is just me), but encouraging your team to get to know each other, inside and outside of work, can be an effective way to build trust within the team. Staff room chats, cups of tea made for parents' evenings, chats on gate duty, or after-work social events can give staff members the opportunity to deepen friendships by learning more about each other's personalities, family dynamics, stresses and strains whilst developing empathy and understanding (the glue you will need when external pressures place strain on working practice and relationships).

This is why, awkward or not, always being genuine and authentic when communicating is crucial – for all staff, including you. It is why you must model this, unashamedly. If staff don't think you are speaking from the heart, any trust they are beginning to develop in you, or have in you, based on acts/decisions taken, will evaporate. The more comfortable your team feels around you, the more likely they are to trust you and want to work for and with you. Fact.

Creating an inclusive culture, the curation of individual and organisational traits that create the lived experience of staff and therefore define your school is perhaps the biggest responsibility you have as a leader. It sets the tone for every interaction with staff, inevitably, but pupils and their parents, too.

Key takeaways

1. Tell stories of success at staff meetings, to reinforce the feeling that the school is moving forward.

2. Discuss as a team the team behaviours which you aspire to – and which the team will challenge.

3. Ensure that you have created enough psychological safety to ensure staff feel they can openly express vulnerability.

4. Communicate clearly and directly – but also with high levels of personal care for the individual

5. Avoid any conversations which lapse into shaming or blame of an individual.

Reflection tasks

Think about staff behaviours which you see around your school. Which champion your school values and which run counter to it (and you would seek to change)?

Behaviours to celebrate	Behaviours to challenge

List the ways in which your staff can give you feedback, both formally and informally?

_____

_____

_____

_____

Think of the last 5 interactions which you've had with staff which may have involved difficult messages. Where on Kim Scott's model of Radical Candour would you place each?

_____

_____

_____

_____

What three actions could you take to improve communication and wellbeing amongst your team?

i. _____

_____

ii. _____

_____

iii. _____

_____

Chapter 9

Working with parents

An imperfect guide

'We cannot deny our love for each other any longer!'

The letter had come amongst the usual marketing circulars and diktats from the DfE.

'The way you chose my favourite song for assembly…'

Chesney Hawkes' 'The One and Only'… I didn't think that was anyone's favourite song?

'The secret messages you hide in the homework instructions…'

I had literally nothing to do with issuing homework instructions.

'The long, lingering glances we exchange…'

I couldn't even picture the author of the letter let alone think of a time when we'd ever talked. Maybe I'd said hello on the gate a couple of times?

'I know you live on [insert road name]. Maybe we could have some fun together…?'

This wasn't in the NPQH!

There was no critical incident scenario which outlined the correct response to amorous advances from random parents! This really wasn't something I'd been expecting on an idle Tuesday in March, about a year into my first headship. I had SATs to worry about! And Ofsted! And the leaks in the roof!!

But who do you call when this sort of thing happens? The Chair of Governors? The LA's commissar? My wife! I was pretty sure each would have an opinion on how to handle this 'delicate situation'…

At that moment, Sharon, the Business Manager bowled in.

'Morning Simon, you OK…? You look a bit pale?'

*

You are a leader of your community

As school leaders we are the captains of the only public institutions which interact with the nation's families for 192 days of the year. We know the families within our communities better than any other civic institution.

Better than the local doctor.

Better than the local council.

And, for most, better than the local priest.

Just let that sink in for a moment…

There is literally nobody who has more of a hands-on role in the family than the local school.

You are a community leader (whether you want to be or not).

As headteacher, you take on this mantle. This is something which sometimes Heads fail to grasp whilst trying to get hold of the myriad of other worries about Ofsted and test scores and budgets and leaky roofs.

But the part we play in the lives of hundreds of families should not be underestimated. We see our families at the best and worst of times. We see them struggle and thrive. We see them grow and change. We will walk alongside them for many years. Sometimes they will be happy; sometimes they will be sad; sometimes they will be enthusiastic about the school – other times they will be grumpy or cross. It is the lot of any public servant in a public facing role. It is a privilege – but one that sometimes weighs heavy. And after a decade or more of austerity and cuts in public services (including the preventative children's services which once caught families in crisis), and after a decade where those in power have stoked division to capture a few votes, relationships between parents and the public institution which is school are more fragile than ever.

But if we are cursed to live in interesting times, we must exercise the power and influence which our position allows to create a vision of a more hopeful, more cohesive and more optimistic future for our families. Like it or not, we have the power, and increasingly the moral obligation, to set an ethos and culture which extends beyond the school gates. In a world where the constant bombardment of opinions leaves parents often confused and uncertain, it is schools that can provide a trusted voice amongst the chatter.

So, as a school leader, we must be clear what we think about a whole host of community issues and then be brave enough to confidently articulate a view of education and community which inspires our families not only to trust us, but also to believe that our society, and their community, can and must improve.

We can't fix all of society's problems. But we can use the tools at our disposal to support our communities to be the best they can be.

So, first of all, you must accept that 'community leader' is part of your job.

A headteacher needs to be seen to be believed

Everyone working in a school knows that their personal authority comes from the interactions which they have with pupils and parents.

As all school leaders were once class teachers, the interactions with pupils comes easy – it's what we've always done. But the interactions with parents can feel new, and at times overwhelming, when we first lead a school. We become the highest point of authority, requiring us to interact with parents in ways which we previously didn't need to.

It is us who rings a parent to tell them that we have a safeguarding concern and will be contacting Social Services. It will be us who calls to discuss bullying, or a racist remark involving their child. It is us who has to deal with short-tempered dads parking in the staff car park on a rainy Tuesday in February. We are the face of the school. The person who carries the can and owns an invisible 'shit hoover' to clean up the mess which is often left in others' wake.

If you have been a headteacher for a while, you will have built up cash in the Bank of Good Will which comes from the parents having known you a long time. But as a new headteacher, you start with an opening balance in the bank of zero. Parents don't trust you because they don't know you. They aren't being mean – it's just human nature.

So all headteachers, whether new or long-standing, need to be seen by the public they serve in order to build up social currency. They need to be seen stood on the gate every morning and every evening; seen at the PTA quiz; seen at every performance; seen at every parents' evening; seen at the side of the pitch when the school team plays a match. It may seem like a huge drag on your time when you have a gazillion emails to respond to, but at each of these events we earn social currency; we gradually accrue deposits in the Bank of Good Will. So when it comes to having to make that difficult phone-call, there is at least some trust and good will to draw upon.

Communicate regularly, and over multiple channels

Whilst some 'soft power' can be developed through simply being visible and clear, 'hard power' – by which I mean the ability to shape the views of the parental community – comes from a clear and prioritised communication strategy.

The first item of business in your communication strategy will be the weekly (yes – weekly) school newsletter. I am still surprised how few headteachers prioritise writing a newsletter which goes beyond simply sharing dates, and occasional reminders. Newsletters are a golden opportunity to shape the narrative. It is your weekly opportunity to bang the drum for the things you are proud of or want to develop. It is a place where the vision, through a thousand words and photographs, becomes a reality in the parents' eyes. It should be a place of inspiring and rousing stories from the week just past: of moments of joy, or where learning is celebrated. It should be deliberately 'tabloid' and accessible in its style, littered with colourful images of successful learners. And as headteacher, this should be a job which you and you alone take responsibility for.

Next, the power of social media should not be ignored (as it still is in many schools). The newsletter will hit some, but not all of the parental community. Social media channels will have a much better chance of engaging harder to reach families in the life of the school. Again, these posts should not be bland messages using stock images, but authentic (ideally daily) content from around the school, once again celebrating achievements and signposting their link to the wider school vision. At my schools, we are currently experimenting with Instagram Reels – short one-minute monologues straight to camera from myself and the other leaders, explaining key aspects of the school's vision. We do this because we know that we must 'go where the parents are'. And our feedback shows us that a one-minute reel is likely to be seen by more parents, and more hard-to-reach parents, than a half hour workshop in the hall on a Wednesday evening. And whilst plenty of heads will balk at the idea of appearing on camera as 'school influencers', sometimes we have to just swallow our nerves and give it a go!

We must communicate in ways which parents feel comfortable with. The EEF's own research (2016) into the use of texting to communicate with parents found that this was a high-impact, low-cost way of reaching parents which drove better engagement than letters or emails.

Finally, we must communicate the good as consistently as we do the bad and the bland. We must be as quick to pick up the phone and tell a parent that their child has done something amazing as we are when they have made a poorer choice.

But failing to have a communication strategy at all will only result in lost opportunities to connect.

Empathise – but don't pity

The excellent Marc Rowland, researcher for the Unity Trust and EEF, describes one of the problems with supporting disadvantaged families as being that most teachers (and leaders) had the same middle class up-bringing, and therefore struggle to identify with a family life which differs to their own. We create a Guardian-reading group-think, which can lead us to judge, and then pity, disadvantaged families.

This then creates a deficit model where all such families need to be pitied and then 'fixed' – and by 'fixed' we mean made like 'us'. It ignores the strength and love which exists. It fails to build on the hopes and dreams of the families we serve.

Instead we must seek to understand how our community thinks and acts, and then build provision from this standpoint, looking to overcome the (often practical) barriers and worries which prevent disadvantaged children from getting the most out of life in our schools. We must answer the question: does our vision serve all, or does it serve *some*? In answering this question we will start to think creatively about how we can make our school truly inclusive, often through small considerations and tiny kindnesses.

We mustn't coddle or indulge our families – we are professionals and should voice an opinion about aspects of family life which may be damaging or not in a child's best interest. Indeed, this is just as damaging as ascribing a child's level of potential based on their Pupil Premium status. But we must balance this with a genuine understanding for the different approaches to life which will be present in our community.

As Marc Rowland notes, 'Supporting disadvantaged families is a privilege, not a problem to be solved!'.

Ask for regular feedback

Whilst obvious, it is still worth mentioning: the only way we will know how well we are serving our families is to ask them.

Most schools will hold an annual parents' survey and this is a great way to plot changes in attitudes over time (at Blackhorse we have asked the same questions for the last 14 years). We deliberately remove the 'neither agree nor disagree' option, as we find this gives a truer (if more black-and-white) picture of how parents feel. We also publish all the results, and every comment (redacted to remove any specific staff or pupil names), good or bad, on the school website, along with our own response outlining what we intend to do in light of the feedback we receive.

However, useful as this formal feedback is, informal ongoing feedback can also be hugely informative. Parents' forums, a termly open meeting with an open agenda aimed at ironing out the kinks in how the school is operating, allow little problems and frustrations to be dealt with quickly in a solution-focused environment. Likewise, parent focus groups on specific subjects, such as diversity within the curriculum, sex and relationship education or digital safety, can also allow parents to feel heard when the school is planning potentially controversial changes.

Don't scrimp on family support

Undoubtedly the roles in schools within our society have changed dramatically in the last twenty years.

We have gone from being 'just' the providers of education to the child, to family 'first responders', picking up the slack which historically would have been managed by a myriad of children's services. The rights or wrongs of this can be argued about on another day, but as this fact does not look set to change any time soon, we must ensure that we have staff available to provide this early help.

Again, historically, this role would have been done part-time by an existing teaching assistant within the school. However, over time the need to professionalise this role has become more apparent. With social care services stretched to breaking point, most of the early help has been delegated down to a school level. Again, we can argue about the wisdom of asking schools to lead the Child in Need process – without funding or often even proper training – but this appears to be the place where we find ourselves.

Which leaves us with a difficult choice as school leaders: either fund a suitably experienced family link worker who can be the de facto in-house social worker (and in so doing allow the powers that be to abdicate their responsibility to provide this service), or allow our families to suffer as a result of inadequate access to preventative early help. Often this decision will come down to practicalities: do the risks to children's education and welfare in the here and now outweigh the school's ability and willingness to pay for this support ourselves?

Almost always the answer is 'yes'.

Now, of all the schools in the UK which I have had the pleasure to learn about, Flakefleet's approach to their parental community really stands out. Here, their irrepressible headteacher, Dave McParlin, explains how...

Case Study: Dave McParlin

Headteacher, Flakefleet Primary and BGT Star

When we think of schools and a sense of belonging, how often do we really think about our parents and community? This is where the exciting stuff happens.

From celebration assemblies to summer fairs, parents' evenings to performances, they're all just as essential in forming relationships now as when we were at school. We now have so many more ways to engage with our parents, including social media and video calling for those who struggle to get in to schools, or may have been historically reluctant to do so – so let's make the most of the technology at our disposal. Who doesn't want to see pictures of their children enjoying themselves or celebrating a school's achievements? So, welcome them in, in person or online and give them reasons to be positive and control the (good) news narrative.

That said, nothing can beat meeting in person and sharing a cup of tea, which is why a while back we set up our own family centre coffee shop, Strive, a shared space for our community to come together. Most schools are doing incredible things for their children, but know that some of the more significant challenges happen at home and out in the community, on an evening and at weekends. We are now able to help parents get back into employment, assist with housing issues or signpost towards mental health support which is starting to have an impact on the children in school. We offer a wide range of activities for our families, such as baby sensory, family trips or one-off events such as Taylor Swift nights or screening the football – and good old bingo still goes down a treat. We love an excuse to come together and inspire positivity, hope and optimism.

For those who aren't into their coffee shops or social media, we have found that some parents love to get stuck into a project that they know will make a difference to the children in our care. Whilst making costumes and doing hair and make-up for our ridiculous Britain's Got Talent journey might not be everyone's cup of tea, we were inundated with volunteers and wheelbarrows when we needed 30 tonnes of sand moving by hand from one side of the field to the other for our giant sand-pit. Watching relationships build over the day was a joy to watch – unscripted team-building at its best.

Belonging and parental improvement comes in all shapes and sizes, and what appeals to one person might not necessarily appeal to another. So, get thinking about what this might look like in your school: the opportunities are everywhere and some of the best ones are the unexpected ones that are still talked about years later. Just ask the parents who wheeled barrows all day – it was the making of some parents and their relationship with school – and they were just moving sand!

So now, after hearing from the most popular headteacher in the UK, here's how to cope with periods of unpopularity…

Don't be afraid of occasionally being unpopular

If we are to take on the mantle of community leaders (which we are), then sometimes, in leading, we will have to make unpopular decisions in order to do the right thing by the children who we serve.

And whilst we never flinch in making that essential safeguarding phone call to parents where we have to inform them that we need to refer them to social care, accepting the anger and upset that this will inevitably bring, we may sometimes back away from other difficult conversations for fear of the backlash that they will also inevitably bring.

Sometimes (increasingly) it feels that in the absence of any clear leadership from local or national government, we are all that is left to provide this unpopular leadership during difficult times. Whether it be banning all smartphones (as we just have at Blackhorse), insisting on children arriving on time, completing homework or calling out poor parental behaviours (often on social media), if we don't defend high standards of conduct in our community then poor behaviours will rapidly spread. But as Sir David Carter once noted, sometimes we need to make it clear to parents that we care so much for them and their children, that we aren't prepared to sit by and let them fail, and therefore we feel duty bound to speak out. Even if in so doing we will make ourselves unpopular.

*

But what to do if a parent loves you...?

I read the letter again.

There was no mistake, a parent who I'd barely said hello to was now making all sorts of suggestions which made a newly appointed headteacher blush!

I immediately rang the LA Commissar. She was a scary lady and would certainly now how to manage these unwanted advances… She'd see how serious this was and would either deal with the parent personally or arrange a full LA Rapid Response Team (no doubt amassing around a black Ford Transit under the council offices as we spoke) to manage the matter…

'That's right… a letter… A LOVE letter… She says I'm playing secret songs… SECRET SONGS!'

There was a long pause…. Probably to give the final nod to the Rapid Response Team…

Then a howl of laughter!

It appeared no LA Rapid Response was forthcoming!

So next I phoned my wife… I would have to pick my words carefully… She would no doubt be insane with jealousy…

'Yes… I'm afraid so… A love letter, yes…'

Again, another pause… probably to wipe away a single tear at the thought of her husband receiving such advances.

'…Poor woman, she's clearly not very well. I hope she gets the help she needs…' replied my wife nonchalantly.

Ill…? I was a young Head… with a range of flamboyant Burtons ties and… yes… an earring! Indeed, I had just that summer had a tipsy Reception parent at the summer fair let on that my tight slacks, worn on the open day, were one of the main reasons she'd chosen the school. And yet my wife seemed to instantly conclude that such a letter could only be driven by some kind of malaise!

It eventually came down to a stern letter from the Chair of Governors, who successfully pointed out the inappropriateness of the correspondence, for the matter to be concluded.

*

So remember this: as headteacher, some parents will like you (very occasionally too much). Some parents will really not like you at all (occasionally voicing this too much also… usually on WhatsApp). And some parents will be often simply indifferent.

But we have a responsibility to them all.

Key takeaways

1. Whether you want to be or not, you are a community leader.

2. Headteachers need to be seen to be believed – part of your job is to be highly visible!

3. Supporting disadvantaged families is a privilege, not a problem.

4. Just occasionally, don't be afraid to be unpopular with parents – that's part of the job of being a community leader.

Reflection tasks

Does your vision reach all, or 'most'? How do you extend your reach to incorporate all families within your community?

_____

_____

_____

_____

List all the methods of communication with your parental community and note how high levels of engagement are with different parental groups. Do these channels reach all or 'most'? Re-read your last five newsletters. How well do they engage with all parts of the parental community?

_____

_____

_____

_____

How do staff discuss disadvantage at your school? Are leaders and teachers using positive or negative language to discuss disadvantaged families?

_____

_____

_____

_____

List the most common issues faced by families at your school. List the typical support responses offered by the school. How effective are these in bringing about positive change?

_____

_____

_____

_____

What are you willing to be unpopular about? Make a list of things which you will defend in the face of parental opposition.

_____

_____

_____

_____

Chapter 10
Working with governors

Learning from your critical friends

Sir Hubert Winston-Smythe had been a governor at the school for as long as anyone could remember. By the time I started at Blackhorse he was already well into his eighties and occasionally fell asleep during meetings – usually during the headteachers' report – which one couldn't help but take as a form of appraisal. A retired Oxford Don, he lived in a Tudor manor house (which he more than once allowed the children to visit as it had once hosted Henry VIII) and was from an entirely different age; an age where landed gentry ran an England of Empire and privilege.

He also always had a story, as though he himself was the history of England personified. When news that the school's cross-country team winning another competition came up in a meeting he awoke from his semi-slumber to quip that he'd 'rather enjoyed running as a youth...' and that he'd '...done a bit whilst an undergrad at Oriel... with that other chap... paced him in the thing... got awfully famous after he did... that was it... the mile... Banister... lovely chap...'. And on that bombshell he went back to his semi-snooze, as though helping to break the four minute mile world record was what all 'Oxford chaps' did.

He would also always be on hand to help with interviews – sometimes offering before other, possibly more 'suitable' governors had a chance to put their hats in the ring. At one interview for a phase leader he fell asleep during their presentation – which, again, was a particularly savage critique of what was, admittedly, a somewhat dull talk.

On this particular day he was interviewing ECTs along with myself and the deputy. And whilst ECTs do have a habit of waffling a bit in their answers, Sir Hubert had a habit of letting them know this. And today he was taking no prisoners. So as the ECT continued to waffle about something or other, he leaned over to me, sat not three feet away from the nervous young trainee, and in his best (and loudest) Queen's English, exclaimed 'Good God!' and rolled his eyes.

The poor ECT never recovered.

We didn't accept Sir Hubert's kind offers to interview again.

*

Getting the most from governors

School governance is a peculiar thing.

You take a group of untrained laypeople and put them, technically at least, in charge of setting the school's long-term vision, setting the budget (in maintained schools at least), ensuring compliance and being a voice for the community.

To the 'professionals' in the room (i.e. you and I) this can sometimes make for a tricky dynamic as school leaders try to tread a delicate path between understanding the governors' position and ultimate authority, and being the person most qualified to actually do all the aforementioned jobs. But as difficult as this relationship can sometimes be, it can also provide huge benefits, if carefully considered…

Remember: they are all volunteers

Whilst it is easy to sometimes get frustrated with a board of lay-people, it is worth considering that the governing body take on considerable amounts of work and huge amounts of responsibility and accountability for literally no money. Whilst in the corporate world governance is a role which is financially rewarded, in the educational world, these people are offering their time purely through altruism and community (and very occasionally to get the uniform policy or some other single issue changed).

And this is why it works. The governors turn up on cold January evenings to be bombarded with technical abbreviations and jargon, by (sometimes) impatient leaders who (sometimes) see them as an inconvenience. So we need to be kind and nice. Governors offer a vital alternative perspective and are grounded in the communities which we seek to serve.

'Headteachers get the governors they deserve'

This line was delivered to me by a particularly wise old headteacher when I first took up the position and I have found it to be constantly true. Whilst we don't choose the governors (it's kind of against the rules), we do have an important role in helping them to be effective. It is a mistake to believe that the governors sit completely outside our sphere of influence.

Whilst they may get some training from the LA or MAT, much of the work needed to shape them into an effective body comes down to us as school leaders. This starts with the habits which we encourage them to adopt and the standards of public office which we want them to uphold. If we expect our governors to consistently act in accordance with the Nolan Principles of standards in public life (selflessness, integrity, objectivity, accountability, openness, honesty and leadership) then we must explicitly model these and train our governors with these in mind.

Most governing bodies contain long-standing members who will have already established this culture and have formalised habits already in place to carry out all of their other strategic oversight roles. However, more than once, and completely by chance (and sometimes quite out of the blue), there will be a sudden turnover in governors, resulting in a new board with few long-term governors with experience which the new recruits can draw upon. Likewise, often governance practices may occasionally need to be refreshed and, again in the absence of an experienced Chair, it may fall to you to support the board in coming up with new ways of working.

Katie Hague gives a brilliant example of how she and the governors at her school worked together to help develop the skills of the Board.

Case Study: Katie Hague

Executive Headteacher, The Orchards Federation, Bolton

I was never going to be a headteacher. Partly because I loved teaching and partly because I had a blueprint in my head that I didn't match. The headteachers I'd worked for had all been (or at least seemed to be!) very confident people who had the kind of charisma that could hold a room. I didn't see myself like that. But then my headteacher left, and nobody applied. It turns out that a 'satisfactory' school in a deprived area with high numbers of EAL wasn't an attractive proposition. So the Governors asked me to be Acting Head whilst they re-advertised. And nobody applied again. By the third round of recruitment, I'd been doing it for a while, including for an Ofsted monitoring visit, and decided I might like it after all. That was the start of a 10-year journey. It turns out that knowing your stuff, being fair and consistent, and building your staff alongside yourself is just as effective as that elusive charisma. And the bits I loved about teaching children – spotting their talents, supporting new learning and bringing them to those lightbulb moments – I applied to my staff team and got the same satisfaction. I love my job.

As a new headteacher who was never going to be one, I hadn't had any relevant training. I didn't do my NPQH and so had to find my way with the help of some hugely supportive colleagues and my governors. School governance is a funny thing. The biggest volunteer body in the country, asked to give their time and skillset to be able to support and challenge schools, without worrying about the operational aspects. They can bring perspectives that we would never think of. I value the job so highly that I persuaded my husband to volunteer at our local secondary school. But how do you get to the point where the working relationship really is providing that support and challenge?

Our school had been inadequate when I first joined, and the Governing Board had undergone a lot of change. Some highly experienced governors had been drafted in to support a passionate and long serving set of foundation governors from our local church. They gave generously of their time but hadn't had much training on holding the school to account. One of them infamously asked 'What does SEND mean?' at a meeting. He was the SEND governor. I spent hours writing reports for meetings, which very few people ever read in advance, and even fewer asked me any questions about. I was getting increasingly frustrated with wasting my time writing things that weren't being read, and with being criticised on every LA review that my governors weren't asking enough questions. So I started using track changes in my word documents and annotating key sentences with 'you may want to ask me a question about this'. It took time, but a broader range of governors did start to do so. This then led to some more genuine questions, which really did make me think.

Governor CPD is also really tricky to manage. Again, they're volunteers and there's a limit to how much time people have to give. I've been lucky enough to work with some highly knowledgeable and committed governors. Some manage to find the time for training but others find it harder – life gets in the way. What I realised is that I could deliver a lot of the training needed to support them in their job. I could do sessions on how to read published data, or the role of governors in looking at PPG or SEND, or web filtering and monitoring. We agreed to 'start' governors' meetings half an hour early so that we could do some training before the main meeting. This was much easier for governors to commit to and meant that we could really target the aspects we needed.

Targeting the time and support of governors is really important. Their time is finite, so what would benefit you and the school the most? Do you really want them coming to meeting upon meeting, or coming in to speak to staff and children? How can they help you bridge any gaps with your local community? Shine a spotlight on the bits that are most useful and ask them how they can get involved. Don't be scared to be honest with them, and ask for help when you need it. They're responsible for your workload and wellbeing, and none of us are superhuman.

I'm really proud of the working relationship I built with my governing board. They were able to support our school on the journey to Ofsted 'Good', accreditation from various national bodies, a local Highly Commended school of the year and a National Pearson silver award.

Use the governors' wider experience

Whilst the governors aren't (and shouldn't be) educationalists, it is wrong to discount their other work experiences. These can be a board's greatest assets.

Governing boards usually complete a skills audit annually, where they outline the skills which could be of use to the team. It is worth paying close attention to this as any one of them could provide a vital specialist advice and insight to any number of school issues. Business people often have a keen eye for the bottom line in terms of outcomes (as well as a keen nose for bullshit). Those with a background in audit or buildings will be of tremendous use when it comes to estate management. And parent governors are often best placed to let you know how a particular decision or initiative is landing on the playground.

Combined, these skillsets can shift your thinking away from lazy educational group-think, which can infect our industry as much as any other.

Governors and the school's vision

Governors technically decide the school's vision – so make sure they have buy-in.

As we discussed, getting the vision right is the first job of a school leader. However, you don't have free rein here, as the governors technically have a significant say in what the school's vision is. It is therefore essential that you work hard to ensure that the governors' vision for the school, and your own, and the rest of the community's, is aligned. You therefore need to have included them in any re-visioning process, inviting them to any INSET days where re-visioning is taking place. Indeed, by getting them to work alongside the staff, and ideally parents as well, during the early stages of re-visioning, you can often gain valuable alternative perspectives which may have been lost in the echo chamber of a staff-only event.

And once the vision is set, it is worth making constant reference to this at all governor meetings, bringing every decision, every initiative back to these core principles so that the governors are able to draw a straight line in their minds between the original vision and the action or activity being proposed.

Explicitly link the work of the Board to your SDP writing cycle

As mentioned previously, one of the governors' duties is to lead on long-term strategy development. However, their ability to complete this function well will depend on the systems and processes which are in place to make their job of holding you to account (and that is their job – more on this later) clear and transparent.

As we discussed in previous chapters, clear, unambiguous SDP targets, with clear unambiguous actions and milestones are at the heart of all school improvement. If your plans and desired outcomes are clear, then communicating these to governors is simple. If they are woolly and vague, then this will be a far more difficult proposition.

When I present the following year's SDP to governors, I do so as a working document and invite requests for clarification and re-wording. Not only does this sharpen the targets and milestones and ensure that they are clear and measurable, but it also ensures that I'm not trying to hide woolly thinking behind big words and impenetrable 'pedagogic-babble' (something tired minds tend to reach for when we don't actually know what we're trying to achieve). Better still, get this interrogation clearly recorded in the minutes – Ofsted love that sort of thing!

Provide a suggested monitoring plan

Governors often struggle to know how to effectively monitor school improvement, particularly in areas where there is little hard data with which to make comparative judgements. Again, it is a mistake to leave the governors to their own devices and to hope for the best – remember, they are lay-people!

Providing them with a monitoring schedule which lays out the milestones and gives suggestions as to how they can effectively monitor these proposed improvements provides both direction and professional growth opportunities for the board. How this looks will depend on the experience and confidence of the board, but some support in this area is nearly always welcome.

Always tell the truth

There is a temptation to try and present an overly-optimistic view of the school to school governors, which over-eggs the strengths and varnishes over the weaknesses. I get it – you're busting a gut to improve the school and the last thing you need, whilst sitting in a cold classroom at 8pm on a Wednesday in February, is to have to justify your actions to the governors. But this is exactly the purpose of the board – to hold you, as the school's leader, to account. Don't shy away from this, and never try to hide errors or weaknesses or failures. As mentioned in earlier chapters, counterintuitively, leaders who are self-critical and who are always looking for how things could have been done better, are the leaders which most people who have the most confidence in.

Obviously, there are some areas which are confidential, involving HR or particular pupils, and you must never cast blame on staff members to the Board when things go wrong (as Head, everything that happens in that building is technically your fault). Likewise, there is a difference between honesty and self-pity and 'over-sharing' your worries (the governing body aren't your therapist).

But honesty allows you to bring your authentic self to meetings and is a foundation stone in forming a trusting relationship.

Cultivate a great working relationship with the Chair of Governors

I have been fortunate enough to work with some superb Chairs of Governors over the years. The last long-term Chair who I had the pleasure of working with was a retiree called David Rowe who had a lifetime of experience in high-level accountancy and entrepreneurship. He is exactly the kind of OAP which we all hope we'll end up be: interested in everything (he took up the saxophone aged 67), keen to make a difference for children who he had no connection with and, most of all, wise. He had seen and done a thousand things in a thousand professional contexts and, as such, little fazed him. Even as an experienced headteacher, his counsel was always most welcome, usually because he had been around long enough to have seen that failures fade in a way that triumphs don't. He could always add perspective, even if I sometimes didn't like the advice he was dispensing. Most of all, despite the healthy professional challenge, I always felt that he 'had the school's back'.

A good Chair is part 'work dad/mum' and part priest. They are sometimes the only person outside your SLT with whom you can be professionally vulnerable. It is often they who you will pick up the phone to when there is a thorny complaint or some other issue which has no good solution, only the least-worst one. So, as headteacher, you need to cultivate this relationship as you will rely upon it more than you think.

We don't get to choose our Chair of Governors, and sometimes the relationship with some will be closer than others. But, without exception, I have found that all the Chairs I have worked with have been the first to come into bat for the school when things get tough.

So work hard to get that relationship right.

The sweary vicar

Pat was the second Chair of Governors who I worked with in my first headship, when I was *very* young and inexperienced, in a school which was in *big* trouble and needed to change *fast*!

As well as being the Chair, she was also the local vicar and saw her role in the church school linked to her parish as a critical element of her Christian mission. Having moved from a parish in a tough London borough, Pat had seen a great many things and wasn't the least bit frightened of anyone or anything.

At the time the parent body were often 'spiky' – offering support to me as we, little by little, turned the corner, but also not yet clear about what was and wasn't allowed in the 'brave new world' of the school's reinvention. Parents would sometimes behave badly towards one another in the playground (more than once I was called to break up physical fights between grown adults), and we needed to establish a clear 'zero-tolerance' to parental behaviours which sat outside the values which we were trying to live by. The incident which instigated my call to the Rev Pat for advice involved two dads squaring up to each other in the narrow EYFS corridor, firing volleys of abuse at one another, whilst dozens of Reception children milled around their ankles. I'd turfed them out of the building at the time, but I phoned Pat for advice as to how to managing this behaviour.

'Call them in – and I'll meet with them,' she replied sternly.

The two dads initially swaggered into my office (this wasn't the first time in their lives they'd been called into a headteachers' office for a telling off). However, upon seeing the scowling Reverend Pat, in full dog-collar and gown, their demeanour shifted significantly.

'Sit down!' Pat commanded, dispensing with all pleasantries.

The two burly blokes, complied, still in shock at this ecclesiastical assault from a small sixty-year-old woman of the cloth.

Pat looked them both in the eye but said nothing.

The two men squirmed in their (ever so slightly too small) chairs.

Seconds passed. An uncomfortable silence filled the air.

'Gentlemen…' Pat snapped in a crisp South London accent, 'Let me make myself very… *very* clear…'

'You will never say "*fuck*" in a Church of England School again!'

The men's eyes popped, unable to compute what was happening.

'Sorry Vicar…' the two figures mumbled, heads bowed like boys chastised at Sunday School.

It was the last time we would ever have to tell off a parent for bad language.

I guess sometimes governors move in mysterious ways.

Key takeaways

1. You get the governors you deserve – work hard to support them in becoming an effective, challenging and supportive group.

2. Use your governors' skills and knowledge from beyond the field of education to avoid staff 'group-think'.

3. The vision belongs as much to them as you – make sure they have a hand in shaping it, and then over-communicate it to them at every opportunity.

4. Use them to sharpen your SDP by inviting critique. Then help them to effectively monitor its impact by providing them with a suggested monitoring plan.

5. Develop a close working relationship with the Chair – they are often your only confidant in tough times.

Reflection tasks

Ask your governors to provide you feedback on which parts of the SDP they feel have clarity and which need further work.

How close is your relationship with your Chair of Governors? How well do you feel they support and challenge you? How could this relationship be further improved?

_____

_____

_____

_____

What aspects of the work of your governing board would you want to improve? How could you go about supporting them to improve in these areas?

_____

_____

_____

_____

How honest do you feel you can be with governors about school issues? What acts as a barrier to honest dialogue? What can you do to improve this?

_____

_____

_____

_____

Chapter 11

Strategic financial planning

Making the money add up

I hadn't slept properly for days.

We'd been through it with the finance officer over and over.

There simply was no other way.

I glanced at the clock. I couldn't put it off any longer.

I stood up from behind my computer and took a breath.

In a matter of minutes an excellent member of staff would learn that I'd taken away their livelihood.

I opened the office door and headed down the corridor.

*

Strategic financial planning

Most school leaders don't go into the role of headteacher because of a deep love of school finance.

A few maybe… the same sort who enjoy Health & Safety compliance courses… you know the sort… just a bit weird.

It is for most new school leaders the thing that worries them the most, as it is probably something most have zero or little experience of prior to taking up the role. Yet, for the main, it's more straightforward and dull than we'd imagine. In short, it's simply a matter of allocating parcels of money into different areas – and then making sure you don't over-spend on each parcel. I caveat that remark by noting that it obviously a great deal more complicated than that, but that, if you have the good sense to find and keep an excellent school business leader, then that's all you (as headteacher) will need to worry about.

But if you're going to run a great school, which you are, then you'll need to be able to interact with school finance, albeit at a strategic level.

Start by getting bums on seats!

It's obvious, but in these years of a falling birth rate, it still surprises me how coy some headteachers are about marketing.

If your ability to drive school improvement is linked, in part at least, to money, then you have to make sure that your school is full. Each pupil is worth thousands of pounds, so a full school is a school that then has the funds to do the business of school improvement well.

And this is where we all get a bit British. We don't want to be seen as brash so we avoid overt marketing and instead simply hope that parents will beat a path to our door on reputation alone. Don't get me wrong, a good reputation will drive most of the footfall to your door, but a few quid spent on marketing will make sure that your reach is enough to fill you up.

Potential parents absorb messages about the school over time. The constant drip, drip, drip on the school's social media channels and via stories in the local free papers, hammering a small number of messages linked back to the school's USP, will gradually create an understanding that will stick about the school's strengths within the community.

It needn't cost a lot (fluff stories in the local paper are free) but it is worth spending a few pounds on a nice promotional video and professional photography for the school website. But don't just hire a photographer and leave them to wander aimlessly around the school for a day. Plan their interactions and make sure they capture everything which makes your school distinctive. Likewise, if you're shooting a video, don't drone on about your excellent phonics scheme: parents choose schools like most of us choose a house to buy – partly on facts but mainly on feel, so sell the 'vibe' of the place, not just your excellent SATs results.

Your SBM should be one of your best friends

As we've established, heads don't usually become heads because they love managing money.

Fortunately, there are people in our schools who do love managing money – and can do it a lot better than we can as headteachers. So you must hire and then value your School Business Manager (SBM)!

A School Business Manager is the person on your team who is there to oversee the business operation (the clue is in their title). And yet, I still come across some headteachers who are yet to accept that SBMs do this part of the job a lot better than they can and who insist on micro-managing or meddling in the fine detail of school finance. This not only absorbs a huge amount of time which could otherwise be spent on the business of school improvement (the bit you're actually good at) but it also serves to annoy the SBM, who will feel disempowered by this.

You need to delegate the oversight of the budget to this skilled practitioner. Oversee the budget via monthly meetings by all means – you're still accountable if the money runs out – but empower them to advise you and the rest of the SLT on the implications of spending decisions.

And your SBM should be a full member of the SLT, present at all school improvement activities. This is how they get to understand what the school is trying to achieve in terms of school improvement, so they will be better placed to offer better advice if they attend these.

This case study comes from a school business professional who has worked in every role within a school office. Debbie was my School Business Manager at Blackhorse until, two years ago, she stepped up to manage finance across the new Leaf Trust as the CFO. In short – there ain't nothing she don't know about running a school's business functions! She's a titan of school business – and a great example of where the role can take you…

Case Study: Debbie Beazer

Chief Finance Officer of the Leaf Trust, Fellow of the Institute of School Business Leadership

If there was one thing I really knew I needed to be a great School Business Professional it was to get a seat at the SLT table. Oh and actually a second thing too – move out of the school office!

Now don't get me wrong, the work of my colleagues who work in the school office and others like them is phenomenal. They are the face of our schools, the first person you meet when you walk through those doors and the first person you talk to when you phone. Often the first aiders, the carers of your children when unwell, the shoulder to cry on for parents (and sometimes staff!), the smiling receiver of deliveries and endless unwanted cold calls… and that's before they even get started on the rest of their job administering registers, absences, parental payments, clubs, trips – the list goes on! It's a frenetic and bonkers workspace to be in and akin to being thrown in a washing machine every morning never having any idea what wash cycle you will find yourself on – but regularly feeling wrung out by the end of the day. These administrators, clerical assistants and receptionists are crucial to our schools and I love each and every one of them.

That said, it's not an ideal workspace for the School Business Manager to work in when pouring over budgets, data and staff contracts with a plethora of deadlines to meet!

I was absolutely thrilled when a new headteacher joined Blackhorse in 2011. He'd come from a school with an SBM so I thought 'brilliant – he'll understand why I want a seat at the SLT table and why I need a quieter space to work in at least some of the time'. It wasn't long before I realised there was a bit of work to do there!

When Simon talks above about micro-managing or meddling in the fine detail of school finance pissing off the SBM, this is indeed very true. However, our relationship didn't get off to a terribly good start for me, because every time I asked him a question or how to do something he would say 'ask Sharon /ring Sharon/Sharon will know' (Sharon being his previous SBM). A word of advice – this *really* pissed me off – it was like she knew everything and I knew nothing! It took a little while for me to pluck up the courage and professionally ask him to stop doing that.

Next up, I found him doing a reference request. I explained he didn't need to do any of the recruitment paperwork – 'Leave that to me,' I said. He was genuinely thrilled. I told him he didn't have to do the H&S inspections either – and he was even happier. I could see he was beginning to quite like the idea of this kind of Business Manager! However, when I suggested that I would really like to attend the SLT meetings he took this to mean only the bits about finance – why on earth would I want to be there for the whole meeting, every week? Surely I was way too busy for that and wouldn't find it relevant. No, I want to be there for all of it – the whole caboodle. The strategic stuff, the improvement stuff, the targets, the concerns, the book scrutinies, the weekly oversight of the school development plan – and of course the finance bits too.

On reflection, I realise in 2011 the SBM was still a fairly new concept for some schools. Being an ISBL member, I thought it was helpful to complete the ISBL Professional Standards Self-Assessment and ask if we could review it as part of my appraisal. For me that was one of the defining moments of wow in our headteacher/SBM relationship, that lightbulb moment, that 'OK so I can really see now how this role can really help me as a headteacher to focus on what I am brilliant at and leave the business stuff to Deb. I can see where her strengths are and where I can help her develop.' It cemented that mutual respect and trust for both of us. From that point onwards Simon encouraged, supported, coached, mentored and constantly nudged me when opportunities arose and he really developed my confidence. For the first time I had a seat at the SLT table – every week for all of the meetings. I felt so nervous to begin with not daring to ask any questions, but of course, like with anything, you listen, learn and become curious, and develop the confidence to diversify the thinking and debate to bring a broader vision and not one that is just focused on teaching and learning.

In addition to that, it gave me such a deep understanding of the school's strategic direction and developed my knowledge and understanding immeasurably, so that I could carry out my role more effectively and feel like I'd played a key role in bringing that vision into reality. I understood now why they wanted to buy more books – to enhance a love of reading of course. I could challenge why they wanted to continue with the Family Link Worker at the end of the fixed term contract and come away understanding the incredibly positive impact this work was having on our most vulnerable children and their families.

I am so very proud of the contribution I have been able to make to the lives of those children at Blackhorse and I see the relationship with the headteacher as being absolutely pivotal to that. Working with great leaders first-hand is a privilege and I have grown and progressed in my career in a way I never thought I could.

Oh, and I did move out of the school office. We created a Leadership Hub where both myself and the deputy head worked right next door to the head's office. A place of relative quiet, sometimes (!), a place where I could see the bigger picture, the other side, the day-to-day events you might not see in the school office, and more importantly I could learn from great leaders. I'd like to think they learnt a little bit from me too – the chats about so many things that often linked to strategy, finances, HR, H&S, premises, IT, GDPR – the whole business spectrum. And sometimes it was just a place that offered a safe pair of ears to listen and support at the end of a challenging day (a jar of biscuits and sweets on hand at all times of course). Although sometimes I had to endure football match outcomes, cricket scores, memories of 1990s gigs, bands and vinyl purchases, and sometimes, just sometimes, the deputy listening to the test match on the radio – very quietly, during a lunchtime, just to see what the latest score was!

What an amazing partnership and journey it has been.

You need to plan your staffing strategically

Your staffing will account for upwards of 85% of your total budget (if it's going above this then your wiggle room to do school improvement becomes very tight), so it's important that you take a long-term view of staffing costs.

Unlike running a business, where you can aim to increase your income as staff wages go up, this isn't the case in education. Through pay progression alone, if every staff member stays where they are then they will get more expensive every year. Whilst you should aim to retain good staff long-term (it's one of the best levers you can pull in terms of sustaining school improvement) if nobody leaves, suddenly you'll have an entire team being paid on the upper pay scales, making your staffing bill ruinously expensive. In a big school this is often less of a problem as more staff means more natural movement, allowing you to appoint newer (and cheaper) staff as people leave. However, it is a common problem in small (friendly) primary schools where everyone loves the school so much everyone has been there twenty years… and are ruinously expensive.

It is a very difficult balancing act, but a good talent management plan, where you discuss career aspirations with each staff member annually and give them tailored professional development, can help you keep and develop staff for a time, before allowing them to fulfil their career ambitions by taking promotions either internally or at other schools. This stimulates movement over time and allows you to replace ambitious UPS teachers with shiny new ECTs, keeping your wage bill manageable.

But you'll still need to look at that (always terrifying) third year staffing cost projection on your budget report and be realistic about what you can afford in two to three years' time. By taking decisions about reducing staffing costs in the long-term, savings can often be made by (if needed) just not replacing certain staff when they leave. Whilst nobody likes to cut staffing, sometimes the financial headwinds will make it impossible not to. Generally, people are less grumpy about a school librarian not being replaced when they retire than they are about a redundancy where a much loved colleague loses their job. If you can see problems coming a long way down the financial track, then you can make less dramatic decisions when difficult financial choices have to be made.

Plan your budget spending strategically

If you've only 15% or less to spend on everything other than staffing, then it is essential that you make sure that your money works as hard as it can to improve the children's learning.

All too often, I hear of headteachers who have a somewhat fatalistic attitude to budget planning, usually keeping spending the same in most areas, but maybe adding 2% for inflation. This is *not* financial planning – this is blind hope!

Instead, you must start considering your budget priorities about 4–5 months before you set the budget for the following year. If you have a good Strategic 3-Year School Improvement Plan, you will know what you plan to develop in the next financial/academic year. So instead of just randomly putting a 'few thousand into

Exercise books		Exercise books for whole school (+Special books)	£4,500	Curriculum materials
EYFS	Refurbish and stimulate the learning environment	Replenish outdoor learning resources	£500	Education equipment
STEM	Replacement & upgrades as part of IT strategic planning	PPA / Teacher Laptops x 2 @£600 each + £80 Rob	£1,300	ICT Hardware (not Capital) Ongoing upgrades – reduced
STEM	Replacement & upgrades as part of IT strategic planning	Computer peripherals	£1,000	Educational IT equipment
STEM	Emergency IT contingency	Contingency for emergency repair/ replacement	£2,000	ICT Repairs
STEM	Licences	TV licence	£170	TV Licences – saving share with other Leaf schools
English	Reading Culture and love of reading	World book day, champion home readers, free readers, teacher book pics	£1,000	Books - reduced
English	Reading Culture and love of reading	Additional books for reading stages/coding/ RB SSP	£1,000	Books – Phonics and reading scheme
English	Reading Culture and love of reading	Damaged books – phonics and bookshelf books	£1,000	Books – non-fiction
English	Reading Culture and love of reading	Unlocking Letters and Sounds	0	Educational software and licences – asked not to renew
English	Reading Culture and love of reading	Libresoft Annual Susbscription	£375	Educational software and licences
English	Improve writing	Spell checkers £30 x 12	£360	Curriculum materials 3 per y5,6
English	Improve writing	Picture books for writing	£1,500	Books

books' and a 'few thousand into resources' you try and be as specific as possible about what you plan to spend. At this early stage in strategic financial planning, four or five months out, you start by adding everything you could ever want or need in the coming year, broken down against your SDP priorities.

By doing this you are making considered choices about what you need to spend your money on. As you get closer to the budget setting proper, and you find out what your income for the next financial year will be, you will need to start to trim this wishlist down to essentials (things which must be bought) and desirables (things you'd like to buy later in the year if you found you've underspent on other areas). Whilst some years this is harder than others, due to difficult financial headwinds, it does generally result in the school having what it needs for the coming year.

Build up reserves when the sun shines

Whilst it is tempting to spend nearly all your budget, keeping a healthy contingency is also very wise. If you keep the bare minimum aside for a rainy day, when financial shocks come (like an unexpected and unfunded pay agreement) then you'll find yourself having to make dramatic and painful cuts which people will notice and which saps morale. Better to forgo that shiny thing which you don't really need during good times so that you can smooth out the impact of financial storms when they come. At Blackhorse, a two-form entry Primary, our contingency maxed out at £400,000 (which was a lot). However, when the financial hard times came, we could support three years of in-year deficit spending to smooth our need to make savings without any dramatic cuts.

So always keep enough aside for a rainy day.

Never say 'there's no money'

I have worked for headteachers who constantly told the staff that there was no money. Whilst it may be true that there's not enough money, telling people the school is skint rarely helps morale. Staff should be shielded from tough financial times as much as possible as they have enough to worry about teaching thirty children every day. It's fine to tell staff that we need to tighten our belts and avoid waste. It's fine to tell staff that we have enough money for the essentials – if we're careful. But don't burden them with the (very real) worries that the sums might not add up – that is a mantle that you, the SBM, the Governors, and the SLT must carry alone.

Sometimes there are only hard choices left

I walked down the corridor rehearsing one final time what I would say. I knocked on Claire's door and walked in, closing the door behind me.

Thirty minutes later I would leave having told this excellent teacher, with a young family, that funding cuts meant she would no longer have a job at the school in September.

She loved the school. The staff, parents and children loved her back.

But the money just didn't add up. Good as she was, we just couldn't afford to keep her.

It was my last strategic act as headteacher of the school. I would be leaving for Blackhorse three days later. I could have left it for the new leader to pick up; after all, it was a decision which could have been made a couple of weeks later.

But as headteachers we must pick up our own tab. It would have been wrong to leave the new guy to start by letting good staff go.

Claire and the staff would still drink and laugh and do bad karaoke with me on my last day just 72 hours later.

Sometimes there are only hard choices left when the money doesn't work.

But if you've enough cash in the Trust bank, hard as these decisions are, the team will generally forgive you for having to make them.

*

Key takeaways

- Find and keep a good School Business Manager. Make them part of the SLT and value their work.

- Develop a talent management plan which allows the team to develop and pursue career opportunities. This will help you keep the staffing budget in balance.

- Start your strategic financial plan four to five months before you set the budget. It will help you focus on the right funding priorities.

Reflection tasks

What is your marketing strategy? Do you have a plan (and a budget) to ensure that your school's vision and USP is well-known by the local community?

_____

_____

_____

_____

_____

What is your long-term talent management strategy? Try using Mckinsey's nine-box talent matrix to help you identify where staff are on their development journey.

_____

_____

_____

_____

_____

Create a strategic Financial Plan four to five months prior to budget setting. Identify key spends in the year ahead and rough costs. Nearer to budget setting, decide which are essential and which are desirable.

_____

_____

_____

_____

_____

Chapter 12
Managing the stress of the job

Strategic laziness

I slowed to a shuffle and then stopped altogether.

The marathon training was a familiar feature of my week, but today it felt too hard. I was ten miles from home and the cold March rain was relentless.

The jig was up.

After helping my new school, Blackhorse, back from the brink (the second time I'd conjured up this trick, having done the same during my first headship) the previous year's SATs results were unexpectedly poor, leaving us once again vulnerable. This year's results looked no better. And we'd lost key staff at a point in the school's improvement journey where we didn't have the latent strength to absorb the hit.

The stakes suddenly felt overwhelmingly high. My wife had counselled against betting the family farm on another 'school in difficulty' so quickly after my first, but, consumed by my own hubris and ego, I'd ignored this advice, and, flattered by the platitudes of the LA Commissar, had jumped out of the frying pan and into (another) fire.

The feeling of super-human confidence which the staff and I projected in my first two years in the post, when I could do no wrong, had suddenly evaporated in the face of renewed headwinds and morale was low with staff arguing and questioning the school's direction in general (and my leadership in particular).

And Ofsted were coming… And the school would be judged 'requires improvement' (or worse)… And then I would have to resign… And then I would not be able to make the mortgage… And then I'd never work again… And then I'd lose my home… And then Julie would never forgive me…

My inner chimp catastrophised exponentially. I conjured mental images of cooking Asda no-frills baked beans on a camping stove in a crappy emergency housing B&B as my young children shivered in the corner of the mould-poxed room.

I sat on a muddy verge by a particularly soulless stretch of the A38 and burst into tears.

*

How to cope with the stress of headteachering

School leadership is wonderful but… well… it's a lot!

The daily firefights just to keep the school running (particularly in a small school when you're the only person in charge); the thorny complaints or staffing issues where all you can do is come up with the least-worst option; and constant pressure to drive up standards with Ofsted lurking omnipotently just out of sight. All of these things can at best lead to a few sleepless nights and at worst herald something darker.

Mental illness is often the secret disease that eats away at school leaders and staff at all levels, often not being recognised until crisis point has been reached – sometimes with tragic consequences. Although I have thus far been fortunate enough to live without mental illness, I have, through friends and family, seen it up close and know that it is not something that can be ignored or 'snapped out of'. This chapter isn't for those of you who are suffering with depression or anxiety. My words will no more cure this than a broken leg. If you are living with depression or anxiety, please see your doctor or a properly trained counsellor. These are the people who really know what they're doing. You deserve to feel happy again. So if this is you, make the call.

These words are meant for those of us who live with the near-perpetual sense of unease which comes with leading a complex public institution. Don't get me wrong, I absolutely love my job. It is the best job in the world. The relentless demands of the role are exciting… but they are sometimes also all-consuming.

So if you want to be doing the job happily, for many, many years, as I have, then you need to take your wellbeing seriously.

Remember: you are strong and capable

Very few school leaders arrived there by accident. The fact that you have got this far – chosen to lead a school – shows that you are someone who has earned this position of trust. A wise person once said to me that 'Leadership is confidence' and he was right. To some degree, leadership is a confidence trick which we all deploy to persuade others, and often ourselves, that we (and they) are made of the 'right stuff'.

The first thing to realise then is that the Henry Ford quote (which I've had on my office door on a bronze plaque for the last 18 years) is true: *'Whether you think that you can, or think that you can't, you're probably right'*.

All successful headteachers sometimes have to fake their resolve and confidence because they, like everyone else, have no magic crystal ball to see what the future holds.

We have all found ourselves looking at our visage in the mirror when we need to step up to a particularly stressful task. Willing your internal monologue to tell happy stories about past success, your fabulous ability and general awesomeness sometimes is enough to silence the inner chimp (2012) (who is quick to tell you how terrible everything is).

When staring in the mirror, it does not harm to look for a superhero staring back at you.

Talking of superheroes, there are few school leaders who I've come across on social media as irrepressibly positive as Krystie Stubbs, so here's her take on modelling wellbeing…

Case Study: Krystie Stubbs

Deputy CEO, Inspire Trust, ex-headteacher and school improvement partner

So, I will be really honest, when I accepted my first headship I had no idea it was going to be as difficult as it was. I had had numerous leadership positions in retail, including being a store manager in a multi-million-pound business and whilst teaching had its own stresses, I had never found the leadership aspects too challenging or daunting.

I know now that this is due to a couple of things – firstly I didn't always have good role models for headteachers so my view of the role was somewhat inaccurate, and secondly, where I did have an effective headteacher to learn from, they had shouldered much of the responsibility and stress themselves.

I actually remember walking into my office on the first day after meeting all the staff and parents and thinking – what do I do now? I have to say that was probably the last time I ever sat in my office with those thoughts!

It was during this first headship that I truly started to understand the stress that the role brought about but I didn't understand or recognise early enough that fact that I was absorbing much of this on my own. Looking back I can see there were a few contributors to my stress levels and a lot of these were due to lack of experience and an incomplete view of what true leadership really is.

Perfection syndrome

I wanted everything to be perfect straight away – I am naturally an impatient person, something I still have to work hard to curb today and I did some really crazy things in my first year as head – I did the gardening in the holidays as we had no money for grounds maintenance, I painted classrooms on weekends as our site manager was too stretched, I covered teaching wherever possible as we had no money for supply – basically I tried to do too much. I worked every holiday and most weekends and I look back and know I was not a good wife, parent or friend during this time. This wasn't an expectation from anyone except from myself but it took its toll on life outside work and I believe it probably contributed to the break-up of my marriage at the time.

Don't get me wrong – the school improved dramatically in a short space of time and we doubled our pupil numbers. The question remains – would I still have brought about this change without impacting my wellbeing as much as I did – I believe the answer is *yes*. Could I have delegated more? *Yes!* Could I have asked for more help? *Yes!*

This was a hard lesson for me – when I was asked to apply for the headship at a large 3-form entry primary I was hesitant but I entered into it with a different mindset. My outlook on leadership changed and I became committed to ensuring that none of my staff got it as wrong as I had! I focused on strategically supporting the wellbeing of my staff and modelled this explicitly – when I worked part time after the birth of my third child it was instrumental in showing my staff that it was possible to be a parent and a leader at the same time. What it relied upon was me being more open to asking for help, being honest when it was tough and remaining committed to a life outside of work. It categorically made me a better leader.

Imposter syndrome

I think I spent my first year as a head looking over my shoulder waiting for someone to realise I hadn't got a clue what I was doing, was pretty much winging it everyday and sometimes not trusting my own instincts because the 'last head didn't do it like that'.

What I have learned over the years is that *you* being *you* and being an authentic leader is one of the most important aspects of good leadership – it was precisely that fact that I did things differently, tried new approaches and was creative in my thinking that moved the school forwards to its first 'Good' grading in ten years. I have also learned to accept that I have got to where I am as a leader because I am good at what I do! Listening to my inner cheerleader is something I do more often and I remind myself that I do know what I am doing. I have accepted that I don't always get it right and that is also ok, in fact it allows others to make their own mistakes and to take risks without fear of reprimand.

Now

I now support 9 primaries in my role as Deputy CEO and my work life balance, or the trendier term 'blend', has never been better. I am strict with myself about how long I work each day and I rarely take work home – emergencies yes, but if it can wait until tomorrow then it invariably does now!

I am a better mother, wife and prioritise time for friends and the things I like to do that make me a more rounded person – I recognise that giving myself time to reflect and to enjoy my life is the best thing I can do to be a good leader.

But it is a conscious decision and I have to constantly remind myself not to revert back!

My top tips:

1. Be *you* first and then a leader.
2. Model how to support wellbeing to your staff.
3. Remember that you are not irreplaceable to your school but you are to your family.
4. Leadership isn't always about 'doing' – it is about 'being'.

Wise words from Krystie. We have all heard of a certain brand of headteacher bragging about working 100 hour weeks, only to go pop within three years. This role is a marathon – not a sprint.

Always tell the truth

I have never yet got into trouble for being honest. No matter how bad the news, my staff, my governors, the LA, my Trust colleagues, and even Ofsted, have always treated me well when I have told the truth – no matter how unpalatable that truth is.

Basic human psychology dictates that our brains cope far better with certainty – even if that means bad news – than they do with uncertainty. This means that, hard as it is, you must pick up and search under every rock within your school yourself. In so doing, you will find all sorts of practices and details which at a surface level you will wish had gone unnoticed. But knowing your school is not just the bedrock of school improvement, it is also the foundation of personal wellbeing as a school leader. All humanity is built on imperfection – it is the human condition. However, the thin veneer of perfection is an illusion in even the best of schools. It may well be useful for marketing purposes, on in putting a positive spin on when an inspector calls, but ultimately, we need to understand our school's shortcomings. And then own them.

I am not saying for one minute that you should constantly criticise yourself (or the school) in front of the staff, but showing an awareness that not every plan will work shows a level of self-reflection which is almost always respected by colleagues and parents. In my experience, contrary to what you might imagine, it usually increases the confidence of the governors, LA or Ofsted in you as they can see that this is someone who is honest and transparent.

And telling the truth is a lot less stressful than trying to cover up a mistake (which will eventually be found out anyway).

Get help

Eighteen years into the role, and with a solid reputation for school improvement, I probably ask for help more now than at any point in my career as a school leader.

There is a misnomer that headteachers, and especially headteachers in schools which aren't part of a larger Trust or collaborative group, must chart a course alone and make every decision as a standalone organisation.

If educating young people was simple, then, after over a millennia of schooling, we would surely have settled on a single pedagogy which could be universally applied. The fact is that there is so much that we don't know about the complex interaction between the child, their environment and parenting, the teacher and a hundred other subtle and nuanced elements which collide in a young person's education. So as school leaders we must be ever curious about what helps children learn. We must look for 'best bets' and ask for help both locally and further afield in order to try and craft solutions which improve our schools. We need to be rigorous in our evaluation of others' ideas, and not blithely accept 'research says' as the sole arbiter of what we should introduce in our schools. But asking another school, another leader, a specialist or researcher, to add their voice to your school's improvement journey is almost always useful. Even if only to confirm what you don't want to do.

Get a coach

The problem with grappling numerous, interconnected and highly stressful problems which the job throws at us is that we are too close to the action to really be able to think clearly about the big picture.

As a new HT in a school in difficulty I commissioned a leadership coach – mainly because it seemed the fashionable thing to do. I remember driving to the first (three hour?!) session feeling slightly irritated that I was wasting my time navel-gazing when I could be getting stuff done.

Boy was I wrong.

Three hours later I had answers. And not answers given to me by someone else. No, these were my answers which had been lurking in my brain all along, just needing a skilful coach to coax them into the sunlight.

Leadership coaching helps you unknot all those tricky inter-related problems and see each for what it truly is – a logical problem with a logical solution. They are not your friend and have no emotional connection to you whatsoever. They just scaffold your thinking long enough for the solution to appear. And that lifts a whole heap of stress!

Whilst most new headteachers have access to such a coach, it is something that sometimes more experienced leaders forgo. However, I have never yet walked out of a coaching feeling anything other than clarity and gratitude.

A leadership coach isn't a luxury, it's a cost-effective way to achieve and maintain clarity.

Make plans when the sun shines...

...and embrace the chaos when the storm howls.

As humans, we have a belief which is as misguided as it is unwavering: we believe that we have complete control of our universe.

But we don't.

Any public-facing role like ours means dealing with a chaotic and disordered world. If the last eighteen years in the headteacher's chair have taught me anything it is that shit happens... often out of a clear blue sky... on some idle Wednesday in March. Whilst we can plan for certain eventualities, there will be a 'heap of mad shit' that just happens.

There will be periods of calm and periods of chaos. Periods of low stress and periods of high stress.

As school leaders we need to use the periods of low stress to reflect on how we have managed high-stress in the past and how we will manage it again in the future. Stress is as much part of our job as Year 3 boys flooding toilets and cross parents arguing over parking. Yet we are often surprised when stress once again hones into view.

When the sun is shining and all is right with our schools we should be developing plans and processes for when the next wave hits us. We need to look down the tracks and try to spot stressful pinch-points (be it particularly heavy workload or run-up to tests, inspections etc.) and create a plan to manage that stress whilst we have the head space to do so. When the storm hits (which it inevitably will) all our cognitive assets will be used up dealing with the whirlwind. Having an 'emergency drill' already worked out in our heads will provide us with the mental markers which we will need to deal with whatever is going on. And this will make it a whole lot less stressful.

Indeed, at my schools, we have an (almost minute by minute) response plan for when an inspector calls pinned to the wall, because no matter how many times you've received the call, no matter how much it was expected, each and every time this has happened, my frontal cortex has instantly switched off and my body's biological response has become no different than if a lion had strolled into my office.

So make plans for stressful situations so that when they hit, and you have a drill to follow.

Work hard and then don't work at all

In the UK we have some of the longest working hours in Europe – yet our productivity is amongst the worst in the developed world.

We use time spent working as a proxy for being productive. We feel that unless we are at school early and leave late (working again on emails, etc. once we get home) that we simply aren't trying hard enough. Indeed, I have seen a number of very high-profile school leaders boast about 7am SLT meetings and talk with pride about their staff never leaving school until 7pm.

And it is this that is the cause of the British productivity problem. In working longer and longer hours, our work becomes lower and lower grade. A job that would have taken us an hour when fresh and rested, takes two or three when trapped in the brain-fog of over work.

So, in order to become more productive, we need to start seeing rest and recuperation as an act of efficiency. We need to spend working hours working, and being disciplined about not getting drawn into distractions (a huge problem when we are already exhausted). We need to actually take short breaks from work during the school day to refresh our minds (I won't ask you how many of you work through lunch every single day – because I know the answer!). And then, when we do get home, we stop working completely. Sure, there will be some days when you just have to get that governors' report finished, or answer that email. But this shouldn't become the norm.

We need to become better tuned in to our energy levels and not just accept that we'll be dragging ourselves over the final weeks of every term before crashing for the first few days of the holiday because we have literally worked ourselves beyond the point of exhaustion. We need to work at keeping our energy levels up throughout a term by allowing ourselves opportunities for rest every day.

Get a life

The problem with being knackered is that you stop making the effort to do sociable things because they sound so terribly tiring when compared to vegetating in front of crap reality TV.

But getting out is good for the soul. Getting out on a weeknight is better still.

Spending a couple of hours with friends provides perspective – especially if they are the type of friends who are entirely disinterested in your SEF/SATs scores/Strategic Financial plan.

I'm not saying you need to go out and drink eight bottles of prosecco on a Tuesday night in term time – that is likely to be 'problematic' come Wednesday morning – but a trip to the cinema, the quiz night at the local pub, it doesn't matter what it is, only that you make the effort to do something. Chances are you'll be thinking of every excuse not to go – but you should. You'll always feel better for it.

'Memento Mori' – practise gratitude

Dr Andy Cope, dubbed the 'Professor of Happiness' in his excellent book *The Art of Being Brilliant* (2024), puts to us a somewhat unorthodox motivational mantra to contemplate: one day you will get out of bed for the last time.

One day you will put on your clothes for the last time; drive your car for the last time; eat your breakfast for the last time.

It speaks to a philosophy which dates back to Socrates and the Stoics of Ancient Rome, who would wear charms inscribed with the words 'Memento Mori' which translates laterally as 'Remember – you will die'.

Now, as motivational mantras go, this one, on the surface, may seem to miss the sunniness and sanguinity of a million monochrome memes which flash before us each time we open our socials.

But it is actually a powerful reminder that 99.9% of the things which we spend our lives worrying about actually matter very little when we weigh them against our health and the health and wellbeing of those we love. Dr Cope puts it very simply as *'If you get out of bed and nothing hurts – you're going to have a good day!'*.

Hard as it is when we have parental complaints, or grumbling governors or crap SATs scores, or Ofsted looming and staff moaning about the state of the Year 3 toilets, we need to actively practise gratitude for the things which we do have. By accident of birth we live in one of the richest countries in the world. Even with the challenges our schools face, our students and teachers have more resources and opportunities than at any point in history.

So when you're having a crap week, or even a crap term, practise every day looking around you and naming the things that you are grateful for. Better still, write them down each day in a journal which names all the things that went right, not just the things that went wrong. Spread the gift of gratitude by noticing the good in your team and thanking them too.

Because gratitude is contagious and it spreads happiness through a team like a virus.

Exercise

If a fully functioning and healthy body is our greatest asset (and it is) we, as pampered professionals at the start of the 21st Century, often do little to keep it that way.

As educators, we all know what a healthy lifestyle looks like, but we often struggle to turn good intentions into healthy habits. Park this alongside the fact that it is practically in the headteachers' Professional Standards that every staffroom in the land must have a limitless supply of cake, and suddenly unhealthy habits are so much easier to adopt than healthy ones. But if you're going to lead a complex organisation, often experiencing stress (alongside the many wonderful moments) then you need to take your health seriously.

I know what you're thinking: *I know you're right Simon, but I'm just SO BLOODY TIRED ALL THE TIME! How the hell do I fit in exercise on top of being a headteacher and a partner (and often a parent to a young family).*

The answer is different for everyone, but for me it is about viewing exercise as part of my job. Better still make it part of your commute (I used to run the six miles to and from work 2-3 times a week before getting injured so now cycle every day instead). Some companies allow workers to pop to the gym as part of their working day. But even in the absence of such luxuries, carve out something every day which prioritises your health. Park the car a mile from that meeting and walk the last bit; make that spin class as immovable an object in your diary as a governors' meeting.

As someone who made the decision that exercise was better for me than smoking back in 2002, and who now exercises every day, trust me – you'll have more energy and your mood will be better afterwards (although not before – everyone hates the thought of exercise before doing it).

Because, as Edward Stanley noted: '*Those who think they have no time for bodily exercise will sooner or later have to find time for illness*'.

When you get knocked down – get back up again

There will be numerous times as a leader of a school when you feel it has all gone wrong. Times when you feel that all is lost and nothing will ever be right again. As a new leader this can feel overwhelming and final. But, the longer I do this job, the more I realise that this is almost never the case.

Sometimes we just have to roll with the punches.

Reflect on what went wrong by all means – this is the key to future success. But keep in mind that what seems like the end of the world now rarely is.

*

And having sat on that muddy verge at the side of the A38 in the pouring rain back in 2014 (having a little weep and feeling thoroughly sorry for myself) I quickly discovered my situation wasn't going to change sat in a puddle. I was ten miles from home, had no money. My wife didn't drive – and I certainly wasn't about to ask her or anyone else to pick me up!

So I did the only thing which I could do. I got up and ran the ten miles home.

By the time I arrived, an hour of repetitive exercise had allowed me to view the existential panic experienced earlier for what it was – just that – a moment of panic conjured out of my imagination. It was no prediction of the future, just my chimp brain doing what chimp brains do: scanning the horizon and imagining lions lurking around every corner.

Within 18 months Ofsted had come and gone. I didn't get fired, in fact, Ofsted were very nice and the school came within a whisker of being judged 'Outstanding' (although the wonky maths data eventually made them drop their thinking back down to a solid 'Good'). What had felt like an existential threat turned out to be just another bump along a long school improvement road.

All that stress and worry had been for nothing.

*

I'd like to say that I learnt from that episode and never got stressed out again, but this would be a lie. Truth is I have been stressed out about stuff that ultimately doesn't matter many times as a headteacher – and I dare say I will again. However, I like to think that, with all this practice I've had with stressful situations over the years, each time I encounter one, it affects me less.

Stressful situations, like budget planning or lesson observations are something we can reflect upon and learn to manage more effectively.

And if all else fails?

Go for a run.

Key takeaways

1. Remember that you are strong and capable.

2. You never get into trouble if you tell the truth.

3. Asking for help is the sign of a good leader.

4. Practise gratitude.

5. Prioritise your health and your leisure time.

Reflection tasks

Think of a stressful situation which has not yet happened, but is predictable (e.g. an angry parent, etc.). Create a step by step guide to dealing with this situation with your leadership team, so that you have a rough guide to managing this situation when it occurs.

_____

_____

_____

_____

Consider where you get your support from (formally and informally). If you don't yet have a leadership coach, discuss with governors/your CEO the possibility of this.

_____

_____

_____

_____

Plan two weekday evening activities this coming month with friends.

_____

_____

_____

_____

Write a list of the five things which you are most grateful for. Keep this list in your office drawer to remind yourself about what matters when you're having a crap day.

_____

_____

_____

_____

Consider all the barriers which prevent you making exercise part of your weekly routine. Consider how each of these barriers can be overcome.

_____

_____

_____

_____

Chapter 13

How will you be remembered?

Whakapapa

It was going to be one of the saddest days of my life.

It was also going to be, professionally, one of the most demanding.

It was the day of my grandfather's funeral.

It was also the day that Rob, a headteacher who I'd known for many years and who had danced drunkenly at my fortieth birthday party in my kitchen, and who I would be taking over from (as emergency interim executive headteacher) in a couple of weeks' time, would be sentenced for the crimes he committed on the school premises.

I'd been warned that it would be the main item on the lunchtime and evening news and to expect the press to be delving into any connection that I had with the with the disgraced headteacher.

All social media photos of my fortieth birthday were to be removed to avoid them ending up in *The Sun*.

I was scheduled to have an emergency strategy call with the LA at 4pm, timed to coincide with the long drive back from the funeral.

But for now I stood under an iron sky in a cemetery, which looked out at long-closed coal fields. Scattered amongst the graves were a surprisingly large number of family and friends for the funeral of a 96 year old retired woodwork teacher.

My mother had insisted that his coffin be made of solid oak. Not as a sign of opulence, Frank Birch was one of the most unassuming men you could meet, but as a nod to his love of carpentry – something he'd taught at the same Sheffield comprehensive, alongside my great uncle (who taught metalwork in the classroom next door), between the early 1950s and late 1980s, when he eventually retired.

Here was a man who had devoted his life to teaching. Alongside my mother, Anne Botten, who became a Reception Teacher, and my Father, John Botten, who had become a History Head of Department and then an LA Advisor, teaching had become the family business.

So laying to rest one of the people who had inspired me to become a teacher myself stirred a certain amount of introspection. Of the teacher he was. Of the teacher, and now headteacher, I hoped to become. The obligation not to disappoint those who had gone before weighed heavy on that late August morning.

Towards the back of the mourners, a man in his early seventies caught my eye. There was nothing especially unusual about an old man attending another, older man's, funeral. But nobody seemed to know who this mourner was. He wasn't a neighbour. Nor a fellow parishioner. Nor a distant family member.

He was a complete stranger.

I watched as he bowed his head as my grandfather's casket was lowered into the ground.

*

How will your moment in the sunlight be remembered?

'The past is a foreign country. They do things differently there… and almost always worse.'

I have been guilty of a great many lazy thoughts over the past quarter century of my teaching career. Since walking into my first classroom in the autumn of 1996, I have believed myself to be a very modern chap. As a twenty-something I scoffed at the outdated opinions of those 'old heads' in the staffroom who couldn't get with the vibe of the new (and so very modern) 'Literacy Strategy' and its younger sibling 'the Numeracy Strategy'. As a thirty-year-old headteacher, I scoffed at the 'old heads' in the LA who couldn't get with vibe of RAPs, and Swim-Lanes, and SEFs.

I was down with the '15, 15, 20, 10' Literacy Hour clock in the nineties.

Down with Accelerated Learning in the noughties.

Down with SATs outcomes at all costs in the 2010s.

Down with 'Research-Ed' in the 2020s.

It was clear to me: no teacher before my current generation had the faintest idea what they were doing. They were at best 'tinkering'. The modern crop of 'bright young things' were dragging a backward profession into the light, informed by 'brain science'!

Now, the story I told myself of the school's history (well, since 2011) is that of a phoenix rising from the flames. Of a school which was in dire straits until thoroughly modern Joes like myself and the current staff came along to walk it into the brilliant white light of modernity. Turn any corner at Blackhorse and you will see the vision that the staff and I have carved into the fabric of the building. Baked, like the walls of Babylon, into every brick. Anything that came before this moment, to me, was mere trivia.

And then I started reading the log books.

For those of you who don't know what these were, a log book was kept by all headteachers in the 19th and (most of) the 20th century. They were heavy bound ledgers within which the school leader of the day recounted moments in the school's history with, often daily, posts. Some were benign (numbers of children attending, visits from LA Officers), whilst others captured moments in a school's story which may now only be found in the moment on the school's social media feeds. At the time these were a legal requirement, until, in the 1990s a new government of bright young things ended this requirement, with most schools being asked to send their log books to a central records office where they would gather dust until some other bright young thing had a clear out and put them in a skip. However, some schools, like mine, had ignored this order and kept the log books in the bottom of a dusty cupboard (risking a bright young headteacher having a clear out and putting them in a skip).

If I'm honest, I expected to read about people who offered leadership which was quaint and 'of its time'. Operationally competent, but nowhere near the standard offered by those of us currently standing in the blazing sunlight. I imagined sleepy middle-aged gentlemen in battered sports jackets smoking pipes and sipping tea, whilst opening letters from other sleepy middle-aged gentlemen at the Gloucestershire Board of Education.

But as I read through these dusty tomes, I began to feel quite foolish.

I read of the school's opening in the late 50s, of its rapid growth at a time of huge societal change. Of the new female Infant headteacher (when the school was split into Infant & Junior in 1964) who developed an ambitious child-led curriculum against the backdrop of an educational world even more dominated by middle-aged white men.

I read about the foundation of school library when books weren't a throwaway commodity as they are today. I read about the efforts made by dedicated teachers to ensure that children learned to read. Of teaching letter sounds 50 years before 'synthetic phonics' had a name.

I read of the dawn of computers and the pioneer leaders who made these part of learning for the very first time. Of the school's single 'BBC Model B' in the eighties, then PTA-funded 'CD Rom' in the nineties, and then, in 1999, the school's first computer suite.

I read about a thousand moments in the school's journey. The benign. The profound. The ridiculous.

I read the final log book entry from a valiant headteacher, upon the day of her retirement in 1992, in what would be her final act as the school's headteacher. She bore witness to a life spent serving the community. The changes she'd seen in society, family and teaching pedagogy. The pride. The frustrations. The tragedies. The happy joyful moments where she had seen learning take root.

The log books recounted these tales of lives touched.

*

The stranger at my grandfather's grave

As the committal came to an end, intrigued, a mourner approached the stranger at the grave of my grandfather and inquired about his connection to the family.

'Mr Birch was my woodwork teacher,' replied the elderly gentlemen.

He went on to explain that, having heard about the funeral from a friend, another ex-pupil, he had felt compelled to come and pay his respects to a man who had taught him some fifty years earlier. For a man who, in the early sixties, didn't give up on troubled boys from war-shattered homes and instead bought a broken old car and spent his spare time teaching these boys how to fix it. The mourner was one of these boys, who he explained had learned a trade at my grandfather's side which had provided for him and his family throughout his life. He explained that social media posts had appeared on the school's Facebook page, dozens of them, where other ex-pupils were sharing their fondness for Mr Birch – who had retired over thirty years earlier.

One man, like all those school leaders who had inscribed their thoughts into the log books, had changed the lives of countless pupils forever.

*

Whakapapa

The Maori belief of 'Whakapapa' states that we stand, arm-in-arm, with those who went before us, and those who will come after. It notes that we currently stand in the bright sunlight, as our ancestors did before us, and future generations will do when our moment in the sun has passed.

We are merely stewards of our moment in time. Stewards of our schools. Stewards of our communities. Stewards of the discipline of school improvement. Stewards whose practice will be treated as endearingly quaint by the bright young things who will occupy our offices fifty years from now.

Dear reader, remember this: we stand on the shoulders of giants.

Giants who we often dismiss. But yet sleep beneath our feet.

And whilst undoubtedly more children achieve more in the 2020s than they did in the 1960s, we have gained some (but only some) understanding of how children learn and this work will continue long after us.

But by viewing the profession's past as a quaint irrelevance we, at best, risk not learning from our teaching ancestors, and, at worst, erase the great leaps forward which were hard won by generations of school leaders who were just as dedicated and curious as we are today.

So to all you trendy 'Research Ed-ers'; to all you crazy 'progs'; to all you 'trads'; consumed with the certainty of belief…

…take a beat.

We may currently stand in the sun. We may be experiencing success and validation for our practice given the current metrics.

But look to your left. To the invisible army of teachers and school leaders which came before you. Who read, researched, experimented, refined and developed new practice. New practice which, as imperfect as it was, provided the foundations for our moment in the light. Teachers like Frank Birch, whose 'deliberate botheredness' (before that became a thing), narrowed the disadvantage gap (before those words had meaning).

And then look to your right. The cohort of teachers and leaders which will follow you. Work hard to lay foundations on which they can build. Understand that we currently know but a fraction of how young minds learn. That in 50 years, naïve young leaders will build forward from the ethics and values which you baked into the brickwork of the school system. Stand true to those values and understand that erosion of ethical standards now lays the foundation for a future untethered by virtuous norms. Be a beacon of good in your community which will inspire those who follow you.

Enjoy your moment in the sun. As times it will be fraught with jeopardy; at times it will be fraught with joy. But we need brave leaders like you to be standing in the sunlight, building not just for now, but for an unknown future. So hard as some days will be, remember that what you do matters deeply to our society.

And then get on making your moment leading your school community sun shine brightly.

Good luck.

The final word goes to a headteacher who I have never met – but respect greatly…

Case Study: Brian Walton

Headteacher, Brookside Academy, Headteacher of the Year nominee 2024 and author of *Lessons from the Head's Office*

On Legacy

I hope that when I finally hang up my faded school lanyard and settle into the misty lands of retirement that no one talks about my legacy. If they do it is very likely I have focused on the wrong things during my career, or I have died. I want neither of these things. Leaving a legacy might mean dreaming big and changing the world for the better but too often I have seen powerful people's desires for acquiring symbolic immortality to be a huge barrier to running a successful school. Rather than provide a satisfying end to one's 'life story' and an ability to influence others long after one's death I have seen them cast chains around a school community and make the life of the new head teacher a living hell.

It is only now as I reflect on what legacy means for the school leader that I realise that true custodians do not seek to create a legacy that will be protected as if it was some sacred history. The legacy of a good school leader is to leave the door wide open to transformation and progress. Inheritance should be about the future, not lost in the past.

When I started my second headship in South Bristol the retiring head gave me some advice that I still remember to this day, seventeen years later.

I want you to know about the skeletons in the closet, the things I have not tackled, the things that I am not proud to admit but no longer have the time to sort out. They are your things now... sorry.

What shocked me was I was taking on a school in excellent health within a wonderful community. A school at ease with itself and its purpose. I spent seven wonderful years there. I initially took this advice as the imposter syndrome most school leaders live with on an almost daily basis. The self-doubt that creates a vision that the new leader will spend their time drifting down the corridors pointing, nodding and tutting loudly about what the previous head did, or didn't do.

In many ways schools are very good at ensuring a legacy does not take hold and restrain a school's development. They are pliable places that live with change on a daily basis. The flux of time is ever changing as it weaves its way through the fabric of the school community. People and ideas come and go like the tides that wash sandcastles into the sea. Children scurry past dusty paintings, rickety trophies and photographs of past 'important people' without the briefest of glances because they have far more interesting things to be doing as they get on, living in the now.

A school stuck with the legacy of a previous leader is very likely going to struggle to adapt to the future needs of its community because I have found that history is often a blocker. The, 'we do it this way here' culture. I shudder to think that my legacy would be a force field barrier that the next head teacher would need to overcome just to change the curriculum timetable.

Therefore, we need to ask ourselves, what matters as a leader of a community? If the answer is 'everything except me' then we are probably halfway there. We cannot ignore the fact that the role we have will outlive us in many ways. That is inevitable. In my book, I wrote about an encounter with an ex-pupil – a family that had often been very challenging in my early years as a teacher. When I saw this six-foot-four tattooed shadow call out to me in the streets many years later there was a moment of pause where on one level recognition kicked in and on another a sinking hesitation of 'What Next?' washed over me. When they grabbed me in a smiling hug and said, 'Book of Legends! You Sir are in my Book of Legends!' I knew that I must have done something right in their world. As teachers we are remembered, for good or bad, and that interaction said more to me than the many meaningless Ofsted reports I have had my name attached to which told me about a school I usually didn't recognise.

Ask a teacher why they went in to teaching and I expect you will never hear the line, 'For my legacy!'. It is likely to be to inspire the future generation, to have a career of value or to follow a passion. They will, like the afterglow of cosmic explosions, remain with those who we meet and interact with. What we need to do in our careers is more than warm the hearts and minds of the people we serve. We need to give them purpose and opportunity: an education. That is for their legacy, and it is one that we are very unlikely ever to see in practice. Leadership is servitude. What we do. Legacy is a by-product.

In truth I have struggled with this throughout my own career. I have chased the outstanding Ofsted grade – though I quickly learnt the folly of this, coveted awards, written a book about leadership and at times this has made me uncomfortable and question my own conscience. Why have I tried to create a legacy that in my rawest moments makes me feel like I am desperately trying to prove a point? For a simple reason. There is no blueprint to be the perfect school leader. We have to do things the best and most natural way we can. We may reflect and have regrets but as long as we never lose sight of the reason we became a teacher, or came in to the profession, then we will do a great job as a school leader and that will be a life well lived.

Bibliography

Atwal, K., 2019. *The Thinking School*. London: John Catt.

Bambrick-Santoyo, P., 2012. *Leveraging Leadership*. 1 ed. Hoboken: Wiley.

Bartlett, S., 2023. *The Diary of a CEO: The 33 Laws of Business and Life*. London: Ebury Edge.

Bennett, T., 2020. *Running the Room: The Teacher's Guide to Behaviour*. Woodbridge: John Catt Educational.

Botten, S., 2017. *Surviving the 1st 100 days... Lessons on leading a school in trouble*. [Online] Available at: https://southgloshead.wordpress.com/2017/07/24/surviving-the-1st-100-days-how-to-be-a-new-head-in-a-challenging-school/

Brighouse, T. *Essential Pieces: The jigsaw of a successful school*. [Online] Available at: www.rm.com/education/timbrighousebooks

Brown, B., 2018. *Dare to Lead: Brave Work. Tough Conversations. Whole Hearts*. London: Vermilion.

Carter, D., 2019. *The First 100 Days of a New Headship*. [Online] Available at: www.leadingtogether.wordpress.com/2019/08/14/the-first-100-days-of-a-new-headship

Chavez, M., 2019. *Values Too Vague? Think Principles To Drive Behavior*. [Online] Available at: www.forbes.com/sites/michaelchavez/2019/05/29/values-too-vague-think-principles-to-drive-behavior

Collins, J., 2001. *Good To Great: Why Some Companies Make the Leap... and Others Don't*. London: Random House Business Books.

Cope, A., and Whittaker, A. 2024. *The Art of Being Brilliant*. London: Capstone.

Department for Education (DfE), 2008. *Improving Schools Handbook*. [Online] Available at: https://dera.ioe.ac.uk/id/eprint/2428/7/pri_isp_handbook_0031409_Redacted.pdf

Department for Education (DfE), 2023. *The Reading Framework*. [Online] Available at: https://assets.publishing.service.gov.uk/media/664f600c05e5fe28788fc437/The_reading_framework_.pdf

Dix, P., 2017. *When the Adults Change, Everything Changes: Seismic shifts in school behaviour*. Carmarthen: Independent Thinking Press.

Education Endowment Foundation (EEF), 2016. *Texting Parents - trial*. [Online] Available at: https://educationendowmentfoundation.org.uk/projects-and-evaluation/projects/texting-parents

Education Endowment Foundation (EEF), 2024. *A School's Guide to Implemementation*. [Online] Available at: https://educationendowmentfoundation.org.uk/education-evidence/guidance-reports/implementation

Farndon, S., 2019. *What is instructional coaching?*. [Online] Available at: www.ambition.org.uk/blog/what-instructional-coaching/

Frei, F. and Morriss, A., 2020. *Unleashed*. Harvard: Harvard business Review Press.

Lemov, D., 2010. *Teach Like a Champion*. 1 ed. Hoboken: Wiley.

OKR Quickstart, 2025. *The difference between Values, Principles and Behaviours.* [Online] Available at: https://okrquickstart.com/post/difference-between-values-principles-behaviours

Peters, S., 2012. *The Chimp Paradox.* London: Vermillion.

Pink, D., 2010. *Drive: The Surprising Truth About What Motivates Us.* 1 ed. Edinburgh: Canongate Books.

Scott, K. 2017. *Radical Candour.* London: Macmillan.

Sinek, S., 2009. *Start with Why: How great leaders inspire everyone to take action.* London: Penguin.

Van Kalleveen, M. and Koijen, P., 2022. *Using the Power of the Flywheel to Transform Your Business.* Shropshire: advantage Media group.

Walton, B., 2023. *Lessons from the Head's Office.* London: SAGE Publications.